The glorious doctrines of grace s[...]
Natalie Brand's book on *Salvation*, [...]
magnificent Savior, Jesus Christ. A[...]
about our rescue from death, dark[...]
and communion with the One in whom all our desires and
longings are overwhelmingly filled. I commend this addition to
the Good Portion series to you, which would benefit both men
and women alike.

Aimee Byrd

Author of *No Little Women* and *Housewife Theologian*

Natalie Brand has produced an outstanding book, an excellent
basis for a study group. A theologian in her own right, Dr. Brand
has a thorough grasp of the panorama of salvation and its
constituent elements. She writes in an engaging manner: clear,
incisive, and highly accessible. Her illustrations are superb and
illuminating. Buy it, read it, and use it!

Robert Letham

Professor of Systematic and Historical Theology, Union School of
Theology, Wales

Excellent stuff... Bursting with comfort and joy, here is good
news for all who feel that life has sapped their spiritual energy.
Natalie Brand writes with freshness and vim, acting as a friendly
guide to the alpine wonders of our salvation.

Michael Reeves

President and Professor of Theology, Union School of Theology

In this latest volume on Doctrine for Every Woman, Natalie Brand serves up the 'Good Portion' concerning Salvation. From election, calling, regeneration (and more) to justification and adoption, we learn how we can meaningfully claim our redeemed identity as daughters of a living and loving God. Highly recommended!

Margaret E. Köstenberger
Associate Professor of Theology and Women's Ministry & Faculty Coordinator of Women's Ministry Programs, Midwestern Baptist Theological Seminary, Kansas City, Missouri; Author of several books including *Jesus and the Feminists*

This powerful and painstaking work is a joyous read for any believer – it truly made my heart soar at God's wonderful work and ways. Who knew a book on doctrine could do that? Big, beautiful Bible themes are explained, illustrated and applied with warmth and excitement.

Ann Benton
Author and family conference speaker

THE GOOD PORTION:

Salvation

*The Doctrine of Salvation
for Every Woman*

NATALIE BRAND

SERIES EDITOR: KERI FOLMAR

THE GOOD PORTION:

Salvation

*The Doctrine of Salvation
for Every Woman*

NATALIE BRAND

SERIES EDITOR: KERI FOLMAR

CHRISTIAN
FOCUS

Copyright © Natalie Brand 2020

paperback ISBN 978-1-5271-0302-3
epub ISBN 978-1-5271-0575-1
mobi ISBN 978-1-5271-0576-8

10 9 8 7 6 5 4 3 2 1

Published in 2020
by
Christian Focus Publications, Ltd.
Geanies House, Fearn,
Ross-shire, IV20 1TW, Scotland.
www.christianfocus.com

Cover design by Pete Barnsley

Printed and bound by
Bell & Bain, Glasgow

CONTENTS

Dedicated to the ministry of *Tamar* in Westminster.
A work that seeks to release women captive in the sex trade
with the salvation of Christ.
www.tamarwestminster.org.

Series Preface

The priest pleaded with the young woman to renounce her faith and embrace the Roman Catholic Church. Only sixteen years of age, Lady Jane Grey had been the Protestant Queen of England for nine short days. Her cousin, the staunch Catholic Queen Mary, would pardon her life if only she would recant. Instead, Jane resolutely walked to the scaffold and publicly declared:

> I pray you all, good Christian people, to bear me witness that I die a true Christian woman. I do look to be saved by no other means, but only by the mercy of God, in the blood of his only Son Jesus Christ.[1]

Jane Grey's confidence lay in the sure hope of the resurrection for those who trust in Christ alone.

Ann Hasseltine struggled to make her decision. She loved Adoniram and was even drawn by the excitement of exploring foreign lands. But was she willing to give up all the comforts of home for the dangers of the unknown? Could she endure leaving loved ones never to meet them again in this life? Adoniram Judson was headed to India in 1811 and had asked Ann to join him as his wife. Never before had any woman left America to become a missionary to unreached people. Ann's contemplation of Jesus made the decision for her. In her diary she wrote:

> When I get near to God, and discern the excellence of the character of the Lord Jesus, and especially his power and willingness to save, I feel desirous, that the whole world should become acquainted with this Savior. I am not only willing to spend my days among the heathen, in attempting to enlighten and save them, but I find much pleasure in the prospect. Yes, I am quite willing to give up temporal comforts, and live a life of hardship and trial, if it be the will of God.[2]

Mary King stirred her pot as she contemplated Sunday's sermon. 'Cook' was a faithful, godly woman who not only prepared hearty meals for the boys at Newmarket School, but also served

---

1   Quoted in Faith Cook, *Lady Jane Grey: Nine Day Queen of England* (Darlington: Evangelical Press, 2004), p. 198.

2   Quoted in Sharon James, *My Heart in His Hands* (Durham: Evangelical Press, 1998), p. 38.

up 'good strong Calvinistic doctrine' to fifteen-year-old Charles
Spurgeon, who credited her with teaching him his theology:

> Many a time we have gone over the covenant of grace together,
> and talked of the personal election of the saints, their union to
> Christ, their final perseverance, and what vital godliness meant;
> and I do believe that I learnt more from her than I should have
> learned from any six doctors of divinity of the sort we have
> nowadays.[3]

Cook dished out spiritual food as well as meat and potatoes, and
Charles Spurgeon never forgot what she taught him.

A queen, a bride and a cook: they were all steeped in Christian
doctrine – biblical teaching about God. These women didn't just
endure theology. They relished the truths of the Christian faith.
Doctrine affected their lives and overflowed to impact others.

As women in the modern world we lead busy lives. We may
juggle the responsibilities of work and school and home. We wake
up in the morning to dirty laundry and an inbox full of email.
We go to bed at night after washing dishes, chasing deadlines
and rocking babies to sleep. Sometimes life is overwhelming
and sometimes it is just mundane. The God who sent His Son
into the world to rescue sinners gives meaning to both the
overwhelming and the mundane. He created us to enjoy knowing
Him, and it is in knowing Him that we find both meaning and
joy. Psalm 16:11 says, 'You make known to me the path of life;
in your presence there is fullness of joy; at your right hand are
pleasures forevermore.' This is why Jesus commended Mary
'who sat at the Lord's feet and listened to his teaching' (Luke
10:39). In the midst of a busy household, Mary was enjoying

---

3   C.H. Spurgeon, *Autobiography: Volume 1 The Early Years* (Edinburgh: Banner of
     Truth Trust, 1962), p. 39.

doctrine – Jesus' teaching about Himself and His Father. She chose 'the good portion' and couldn't tear herself away.

How do you feel about doctrine? Do you dwell on the gospel, meditate on the excellencies of Christ and discuss the doctrines of grace? Do you relish the truths of the Christian faith? This series of books on doctrine for women is an attempt to fuel your enjoyment of God by encouraging a greater knowledge of Him. It is our hope that the biblical doctrines laid out here will not only increase your head-knowledge but will be driven down into your heart, bearing fruit in your life and overflowing into the lives of others.

Keri Folmar
September 2016

Introduction

> The LORD your God is in your midst,
> *a mighty one who will save* (Zeph. 3:17).

Salvation in Christ is an epic rescue mission ... and it is the rescue of all rescues! Recently a great outdoorsman told me that in the practice of water rescue there is a 'partial rescue' and a 'true rescue'. The distinction is important. In a partial rescue someone might throw a ring or a rope, or thrust out a branch to the person in danger. With this aid the endangered person still has to help themselves, so the rescue is only in part. One 'true save' is a 'live-bait rescue' whereby the rescuer jumps into the water and takes hold of the person in danger. Here the rescuer gives up their own safety and enters the tumultuous, cold and treacherous water to save the drowning person.

This is the rescue of Jesus Christ. In the incarnation Christ enters into our perilous situation, wraps Himself around us in saving spiritual union, and hauls us out to safety. Here the second person of the Holy Trinity delivers a 'live-bait rescue' at Calvary, bearing the sin of the world in His body, dying a bloody death on a Roman cross. Christ is not a partial rescuer. He is not distant. Jesus accomplishes a true save! It is the rescue of rescues!

This rescue is imperative, for it is impossible for us to save ourselves. Without our divine Saviour we are hell-bound, destined for God's eternal judgement. Contrary to the lies that beset us in our twenty-first century comfort, salvation in Christ is not a spiritual retirement plan because we want to go to heaven. It is not a first-class ticket on a sanctified cruise ship. *We are in the icy water facing certain death … drowning in our sin.* And yet Jesus Christ takes on humanity so He can redeem us. 'The LORD your God is in [our] midst, *a mighty one who will save* (Zeph. 3:17). Like Noah's ark, Jesus is the ark that saves us because God 'has not destined us for wrath, but to obtain salvation through our Lord Jesus Christ' (1 Thess. 5:9).

But what exactly is this salvation? What does our redemption in Christ look like? How does it take hold of us? These questions are the glorious skin and bones of the gospel. Instead of sweeping these truths under a thick carpet that we might call 'mystery', this book explores and examines them with confidence and a thirst for wonder.

Salvation is a Person

Perhaps in the past you have avoided these God-truths. Maybe doctrine makes your head spin and theological technicalities overwhelm you. But theology certainly doesn't need to intimidate us. Doctrines are not dry, dusty concepts confined to weighty books that can wedge doors open. Our salvation is a person: the Lord Jesus Christ. The elderly Simeon testified to this once his long wait for God's deliverer was up. Holding God Incarnate as a baby in his arms, he said 'Lord, now you are letting your servant depart in peace, according to your word; *for my eyes have seen your salvation*' (Luke 2:29-30). What a comfort this is when we feel too mentally fogged up or inadequate to comprehend the glorious complexities of our salvation.

This book has been written (like the other books in *The Good Portion* series) to lead you to biblical truth and worship. In it we will look at *why* we need rescuing, how Christ's death and resurrection *accomplishes* salvation, and how this work is *applied* to us by the Holy Spirit.

As we consider all the gospel graces that make up our salvation, I hope you will agree that 'theology is meant to be *lived*, *prayed*, and *sung*!'[1] I pray that you will be so enthralled with the Lord Jesus that you will sing and even dance over the Lord's lavish salvation! May we be women moved to worship with the Psalmist: 'I have trusted in your steadfast love; *my heart shall rejoice in your salvation*. I will sing to the LORD, because *he has dealt bountifully with me*' (Ps. 13:5-6).

---

1   Wayne Grudem, *Systematic Theology: An Introduction to Biblical Doctrine* (Leicester: IVP, 1996), 16.

PART ONE — SALVATION ACCOMPLISHED

The Salvation Plan and Christ's Accomplished Death and Resurrection

Chapter 1

In Ancient Days: Election

He chose us in him ... (Eph. 1:4)

It was one of those *I-should-probably-read-this-before-I-sign-it* moments. A friend and I had just landed in Atlanta after a transatlantic flight and we were collecting a car from a rental depot. I scanned the contract quickly. One somewhat intriguing sentence caught my eye. The contract stated I was accepting the company's terms that if I drove the vehicle to Alaska, I would no longer be insured. *Alaska?* I thought, *what's wrong with Alaska? It's still the United States.*

Later, after pushing the bulky, white Chrysler into cruise, I thought about Alaska. Then it hit me! Alaska is no smooth, flat Florida beach. There are mountains, valleys, glaciers, forests, ice fields, plains, fjords, bears, eagles and whales. It's wild. It's rugged. There might be rocks on the roads, ice on the roads, moose on the roads. The rental company didn't want me to take their car to Alaska because Alaska is a dangerous country. Magnificent ... but dangerous.

Doctrine is like Alaska. Although many of us would have it otherwise, truths about the Most High God and His glorious salvation are wild and rugged. They are not easy country. Instead, they stretch our minds and worldviews, driving us out of our comfort zones. Our Triune God is awesome, infinite, eternal, unchanging, all-powerful, all-knowing, and omnipresent. Therefore, each doctrine is a mighty mountain range of unfathomable depth and incomprehensible height. The Bible reveals something of these wonders to us but conceals a great deal of mystery. Biblical doctrine is not safe. It is not comfortable. You can't conquer it all. Doctrine is dangerous because it is mysterious, mighty truth about a God far bigger than we can comprehend ... But it is magnificent!

In the exploration of these mysterious mountains of truth we make spectacular discoveries that stir us to worship and transform our lives. Sure, digging deep into God's Word can be strenuous work. But it's more rewarding than we can ever imagine. When we dig hard enough in the Alaska of doctrine, we discover vast rivers of gold! Whereas if you stick to a Florida beach, you'll be lucky to find a lost Rolex.

The Greatest Election

In ancient days before the foundation of the world, the second person of the Triune God was *chosen* to be the Saviour of lost humanity. This was ordained by Father, Son and Holy Spirit in a pact for peace or 'the covenant of redemption'. In His divine foreknowledge God knew we were going to rebel and get stuck into a mess of deadly sin. Peter speaks of this in the council in Jerusalem, 'for truly in this city there were gathered together against your holy servant Jesus, whom you anointed, both Herod and Pontius Pilate, along with the Gentiles and the people of Israel, to do whatever your hand and your plan had predestined to take place' (Acts 4:27-28). The eternal Godhead ordained that God the Son step out of heaven and clothe His divinity with humanity and die at the hands of rebellious hearts. He would be Jesus Christ the Messiah, King of kings and Lord of lords. He would appear amongst a people that God would make His own, and from this people God's salvation would spread abroad to all whom God would choose. Matthew witnesses to Jesus as the fulfilment of Old Testament prophecy for this Messiah, 'Behold, my servant whom I have *chosen*, my beloved with whom my soul is well pleased. I will put my Spirit upon him, and he will proclaim justice to the Gentiles' (Matt. 12:18, Isa. 42:1).

It is not surprising that God ordained salvation in Christ long before the mountains and ancient oaks birthed from the ground. Our eternal God was there. 'Before the mountains were brought forth, or ever you had formed the earth and the world, from everlasting to everlasting you are God' (Ps. 90:2). Salvation started with the Godhead choosing the Son to be Saviour. This is *His* election and the greatest election that has ever taken place. Our election in eternity is based on Christ's *greater* election in eternity. He was chosen first and we were then chosen to be in Him. This was God's 'purpose, which he set forth in Christ as a plan for the fullness of time, to unite all things in him' (Eph. 1:9-10). Therefore, 'when the fullness of time had come, God sent forth his Son, born of woman, born under the law, to redeem those who were under the law, so that we might receive adoption as sons [and daughters]' (Gal. 4:4-5).

So ... as a result ... one warm day on the river banks of the Jordan, a somewhat unusual man dressed in camel's hair, laid eyes on a fellow Jew and cried out, 'Behold, the Lamb of God, who takes away the sin of the world!' (John 1:29). As John the Baptist pulled the Incarnate Son of God out of the water, a voice spoke from heaven, 'This is my Son, *my Chosen One*; listen to him!' (Luke 9:35). His obedience, death and resurrection would rescue humanity from perishing in a godless mire of idolatry and rebellion.

Covenants and helicopters

As the helicopter roared over the city of Brighton, I stared at the soft line of silver-blue sea meeting a speckled beach of pebbles. From the beach stretched neat rows of white and cream Georgian townhouses and grey tower blocks. The view was fantastic.

I had a big hunch as to why we were floating up above the city. Tom had asked my father for my hand in marriage a couple of months before, and I was impatiently waiting for him to pop the question. We smiled at each other in excitement and I turned to the window to allow him to rummage in his pocket. Seconds later, in what sounded more like an ecstatic yelp than an elegant marriage acceptance fitting for a Jane Austen drama, I promised to marry him. It was a commitment to the institution of marriage. But more than that, it was a commitment to marry a specific man – Thomas Brand.

When the Holy Trinity ordained salvation, it was a specific plan to save by means of a specific man – Jesus Christ the incarnate Son of God. Just as it is absurd to think of the marriage promise I made in that helicopter apart from the person I was marrying, it is absurd to consider the Godhead's salvation in election apart from the person of Jesus Christ and union with Him. Theologian John Murray says, 'Those who will be saved were not even contemplated by the Father in the ultimate counsel of his predestining love apart from union with Christ – they were *chosen* in Christ.'[1] 'There is salvation in no one else, for there is no other name under heaven given among men by which we must be saved' (Acts 4:12). Salvation does not exist apart from Jesus.

WHAT IS ELECTION?

Theologians tend to place election within the *application* of salvation (see part two). However, we start with the doctrine of election in salvation *accomplished* because, as Wayne Grudem states, 'it is chronologically the *beginning* of God's dealing with us in a gracious way. Therefore, it is rightly thought of as the first step in the process of God's bringing salvation to us individually.'[2] Election is not the application of salvation but the intention of salvation.

So, what is election exactly? We are all familiar with political elections; candidates are presented and we elect our favourite by voting for them. *Election* is the choosing. *To elect* is to make a choice. The doctrine of election, or the broader word 'predestination', is Scripture's teaching that God chose a people for Himself in eternity past. It is a teaching that many Christians wrestle to understand or accept. Yet right at the start of Paul's letter to the Ephesians he reminds them that they were chosen

---

1   John Murray, *Redemption: Accomplished and Applied* (London: Banner of Truth, 1961), 162 [emphasis mine].

2   Grudem, *Systematic*, 669.

by God, 'Even as he chose us in him before the foundation of the world, that we should be holy and blameless before him' (Eph. 1:4). The Bible tells us that this choosing is not based on any credentials – goodness, intellect or beauty – it is simply born out of God's own love and His will. 'In *love*, he predestined us for adoption as sons [or daughters] through Jesus Christ, according to the purpose of his *will*' (Eph. 1:4-5). Paul reaffirms this, 'In him we have obtained an inheritance, *having been predestined according to the purpose of him who works all things according to the counsel of his will*' (v. 11).

Paul demonstrates that divine election is not due to any godliness (past, present or future) by reminding us of God's choice of Jacob over Esau. God didn't favour Jacob because, as I thought as a kid, Esau was too hairy. It was because of God's sovereign purposes. 'Though they were not yet born and had done nothing either good or bad – in order that God's *purpose* of election might continue, not because of works but because of him who calls' (Rom. 9:11). Moses recalls this choosing of Jacob to Jacob's descendants Israel generations later, 'the LORD set his heart in love on your fathers and chose their offspring after them, you above all peoples, as you are this day (Deut. 10:15).

These verses confirm to us that divine election needs to be framed in God's divine purposes and will. The Trinity's pact of peace emphasises that *salvation in Christ starts with the will of God*. Christ Himself told Nicodemus that new life is given to those who are born 'not of blood nor of the will of the flesh nor of the will of man, but of God' (John 1:13). As Paul writes to Timothy, God 'saved us and called us to a holy calling, not because of our works but because of *his own purpose and grace*, which he gave us in Christ Jesus before the ages began' (2 Tim. 1:9). Whether God's Old Testament choosing of Israel or His chosen people in

Christ, God's election is founded upon His sovereign will and eternal love. His purposes never fail.

Chosen in love

If the redemption story was ever told like the Norman conquest of England, in the 70-metre-long Bayeux tapestry, God's electing love would be a thick golden thread running from beginning to end out of which everything is woven. Throughout the Bible we see God choosing to set apart certain individuals for His purposes and glory. God chose Noah to build an ark and be saved from the flood (Gen. 6:17-18). He chose to make a covenant with a pagan called Abram (Gen. 12:1-3, Josh. 24:2-3). God chose the family of Jacob, from which to build His own people (Gen. 17:19, Rom. 9:13). He chose Moses to rescue His people from Egypt, leading them to a promised homeland (Ex. 2:10). He chose the Levites to serve as His priests in His temple (Deut. 18:5). He chose Saul and David to be kings over His people (1 Sam. 10:24; 16:1). God chose Jerusalem to be the city where His glory and name dwelt (2 Chron. 6:5-6). The Lord even chose a young virgin to carry and mother the incarnate Son (Luke 1:28-31).

It is significant that God chose Israel to be His covenant people. 'The LORD your God has chosen you to be a people for his treasured possession, out of all the peoples who are on the face of the earth' (Deut. 7:6). Yet God says through Moses, 'It was not because you were more in number than any other people that the LORD set his love on you and chose you, for you were the fewest of all peoples' (Deut. 7:7). What electing love! God didn't choose Israel because He wanted a terrible army. As slaves bound in Egypt, they were pretty unimpressive. Neither did He choose them because they were particularly righteous. How many times in the Old Testament do we see them to be selfish, fickle and rebellious? This election wasn't about Israel at all. It was about God choosing to 'set his love' on them. They were special because God chose to be their covenant husband making Israel His bride (Isa. 54:5), keeping the oath that He swore to their fathers (Deut. 7:8).

It is the same for you and me. We are not chosen to join God's people because the church needs our pizzazz and without us it would die out of sheer drear and drudgery. Or because we slave tirelessly away in ministry when others don't. We were chosen because in His purposes, God set His electing love on us. You may be one of those super-gifted Christian women but you were not chosen for your gifts. Election in Christ has nothing to do with the fact that your home-baked cakes and puddings are widely extolled throughout the church. Or your breath-taking flower arrangements leave church members choking for air. Or your worship leading is so angelic there isn't a dry eye for ten miles. Election is about the Lord's glory and purposes. This is good news for normal human beings such as myself. God won't reject me because my bring-and-share offerings remain completely untouched while everyone else takes home an empty plate. Or my church flower arrangement looks as though a herd of buffalo ran through it on the way to church. Or because I won't ever cut the worship group. God has 'saved us and called us to a holy calling, not because of our works but because of his own purpose and grace, which he gave us in Christ Jesus before the ages began' (2 Tim. 1:9). Phew!

Does God have favourites?

My three young daughters are so different. They each have certain charms that endear them; the eldest is so sweet and kind, the middle one has me in stitches, and the youngest is simply scrumptious. Of course, one is not to be favoured above the rest. Such favouritism would be undeserved, unfair and unloving.

Why? Because they are *all* my children, all deserving to be treasured.

One reason Christians kick against the doctrine of election is because it can sound like God has favourites. Surely if God chooses to save some and not others then that, like favouritism in a family, is undeserved, unfair and unloving. But the difference here is we are NOT deserving. If the doctrine of election leaves us with a taste of injustice in our mouths, then we need to realign our sense of justice to God's. God is just. His sense of justice is far greater than ours. His mercy in Christ is never at the cost of justice. For 'none get less than they deserve (justice), but some get more than they deserve (grace).'[3] Election is all of grace and grace is not owed. God doesn't have to save any of us, but He delights to. God cannot show partiality because there is nothing to make us partial to Him. Deuteronomy chapter 10 tells us, 'For the LORD your God is God of gods and Lord of lords, the great, the mighty, and the awesome God, who is not partial and takes no bribe' (Deut. 10:17). Paul anticipates our hang-ups because he writes, 'For God shows no partiality' (Rom. 2:11). Does this mean we are left with an arbitrary election? Does God choose His people in some kind of lucky dip or lottery? If our logic brings us to this conclusion then we are left in a sticky situation regarding the nature of God Himself. However, the whole counsel of Scripture can help us. Does the Bible teach salvation to be the random act of a capricious God? No! The Bible teaches us that God is love (1 John 4:16) and He is wise, good and just. 'What shall we say then? Is there injustice on God's part? By no means! For he says to Moses, "I will have mercy on whom I have mercy, and I will have compassion on whom I have compassion"' (Rom. 9:14-15).

---

3   Bruce Demarest, *The Cross and Salvation: The Doctrine of Salvation* (Foundations of Evangelical Theology) (Wheaton: Crossway, 2006), 124.

We know that *all* have received the revelation of God. Creation declares His glory and power and yet many disregard this general revelation, suppressing the truth by their ungodliness (Rom. 1:18). They are then without excuse (Rom. 1:20).

There is much mystery in election. Calvin wrote, 'Let us not be ashamed, where this topic is concerned, to be ignorant of some things in which a degree of ignorance is more learned than knowledge itself.'[4] We do not know why God chooses some and not others. But we know redemption is orchestrated in God's divine wisdom. As Paul writes, we are saved 'according to the riches of his grace, which he lavished upon us, in all wisdom and insight making known to us the mystery of his will, according to his purpose' (Eph. 1:7-9).

Talking back!

Imagine with me that you have decided to indulge in a craft retreat for a day. You have driven into the lush countryside, paid out an obscene amount of money, partaken in some welcoming tea and cake, and then the time comes for the first activity of the day – pottery. First, showing you how it is done, the teacher effortlessly forms a masterpiece with just her little finger in five seconds flat. Then it's your turn. You nervously take your position behind the pottery wheel, grab a fistful of brown clay, and get to work. After half an hour of shaping and prodding, you give up and place your rather pathetic looking vase (which looks more like a lopsided ashtray) on the table.

Then you hear a small voice clear its throat is an obstinate manner. Looking down in surprise, you see your ashtray talking to you.

---

4   John Calvin, *Institutes of the Christian Religion: Calvin's Own 'Essentials' Edition* (Edinburgh: Banner of Truth, 2014), 463-464.

'How dare YOU make ME this way!' The clay says, getting very cross, and proceeds to give you an earful about its own expectations for its shape and existence. Of course, you would be all astonishment and laughter. What right would a lump of clay have to complain against you the potter? As the creator you have complete creative licence.

The problem with us creatures sometimes is our sense of entitlement. We are but human clay and yet in our sinful pride we are full of *our* own rights, obsessed with *our* power and glory. Although we have been lovingly created by a loving God, made in His image, we want to dictate, rebel, usurp, enthrone!

Paul deals with the same concerns some Christians have over election in Romans chapter 9:

> So then [God] has mercy on whomever he wills, and he hardens whomever he wills. You will say to me then, 'Why does he still find fault? For who can resist his will?' *But who are you, O man, to answer back to God?* Will what is moulded say to its moulder, 'Why have you made me like this?' Has the potter no right over the clay, to make out of the same lump one vessel for honourable use and another for dishonourable use? (Rom. 9:18-21).

Here Paul illustrates, quite powerfully, that we struggle to grasp the truth of election because we limit our sights to our two-dimensional clay world. We refuse to have a Potter-centred worldview. In our myopic me-ism, we cannot see past our own sphere. 'Woe to him who strives with him who formed him, a pot among earthen pots. Does the clay say to him who forms it, "What are you making?" or "Your work has no handles"?' (Isa. 45:9). Thankfully we have God's Word to push us into the Creator-glorifying, grace- and mercy-saturated sphere of the Potter.

Final Destination

When you're driving a long journey, what a relief it is – after hours and hours in the car – to finally see your destination in big letters on the signs slung over the road. The goal is in sight! The Bible teaches us that in our salvation in Christ, we are on a journey to a final destination; and that goal is always in sight. You might ask what exactly is the significance of election? Well if you belong to Christ, you now have that destination. This is why election and predestination normally come together; the three letters '*pre*' mean 'before', so predestination is the 'before destination'. From this we have the word 'destiny'. This pre-destination or destiny is what the elect were chosen for. Paul wrote of this destination in Ephesians; 'he chose us in him before the foundation of the world, that we should *be holy and blameless before him*. In love he predestined us *for adoption to himself as sons* through Jesus Christ' (Eph. 1:4-5). As those elected in Christ, this is our destiny; to be holy and blameless sons and daughters of God. Similarly, in Romans chapter 8, 'For those whom he foreknew he also predestined *to be conformed to the image of his Son*' (Rom. 8:29). The Christian's destination is becoming spotless and pure children of God in Christ (2 Tim. 2:10; Rom. 8:29). We look to our glorification in heaven as full children of God, holy and Christlike. God's plans are not like our plans; they always work out (Job 23:13). What a huge comfort and encouragement to know that God will continue to work in us and bring us through to glory by His Son (Phil. 1:6).

Some Arminian theologians believe God's election is based on His knowledge of the future. That He chooses those He knows will believe in Him in the future. But this is completely alien to Christ's own teaching. Jesus said to His own disciples, 'You did not choose me, but I chose you and appointed you that you should go and bear fruit' (John 15:16). Salvation is all of the

Lord and it starts with Him. As we later consider God's call and His spiritual gifts of new life and faith, we will appreciate this more. But we chose Him because He first chose us. 'We love because he first loved us' (1 John 4:19).

Fiercely Personal

I have a close friend who, in her purple dreads, tattoos, colourful outfits and her hands busy with rings, everyone thinks is a hippy vegetarian. But most days you can find her playing her guitar, eating meat and singing to Jesus. This underlines the fact there is no mould in the Bride of Christ but Christ Himself. The truth of divine election means that God doesn't choose us because we fit an Evangelical mould. Here is the security to be a Christ-like version of ourselves, not a Christian clone. This means the doctrine of election is fiercely personal. Contrary to criticism of this doctrine, we have not been lumped into the gigantic church body, too small or insignificant for God's particular and personal love.

And yet, gloriously, we are a chosen community. Peter writes to the 'elect exiles' in Asia, 'you are a chosen race, a royal priesthood, a holy nation ...' (1 Pet. 1:1, 2:9). God chooses us as individuals, not on our own merits, to be part of His Holy Bride (2 Thess. 2:13). Election should humble us because it is deeply personal, as we are chosen as individuals to be a part of an eternal family belonging to God.

Make it sure!

In our sinful pride we might warp this teaching of election and make it an excuse to take life easy; to rest on our spiritual laurels you might say. But the Bible bids us to 'make our election sure' by striving for godliness. As Peter writes, 'be all the more diligent to confirm your calling and election' with 'godliness,

virtue, knowledge, self-control, steadfastness, affection and love'
(2 Pet. 1:5-7, 10). Samuel Rutherford says powerfully in one of
his letters, 'God knows that you are his own. Wrestle, fight, go
forward, watch, fear, believe, pray; and then you have all the
infallible symptoms of one of the elect of Christ within you.'[5]
The believer has been prized by God's saving grace in Christ
before time began. This is the most humbling reality that you
and I will ever personally know. Squandering this will only lead
to uncertainty of election. Safeguarding our election in holiness
and enjoyment of Christ will only confirm it.

This awesome doctrine also gives us comfort. Have you ever
thought that God might reject you because of your sin or cold
heart towards Him? Sometimes in our mess we hesitate to turn
to God because we are afraid of being shunned. The wonder of
election is this, God will never reject you when you call upon
Him. The Mighty Godhead chose you for Himself long before
He called creation into being! The Lord Jesus said, 'All that the
Father gives me will come to me, and whoever comes to me I
will never cast out' (John 6:37).

Conclusion

Election is a difficult doctrine for us to grasp, but we cannot
allow what is comfortable to shape our theology. We cannot
swipe left on biblical truths, like they are unwanted pages on our
tablets. Don't want the doctrine of hell? Swipe! Or humanity's
total depravity? Swipe! These are the doctrines of our Holy
awesome God. They have little to do with our comfort. We must
accept, treasure and teach every biblical doctrine, and not shrink
from declaring 'the whole counsel of God' (Acts 20:27).

---

5   Samuel Rutherford, *The Loveliness of Christ* (Edinburgh: The Banner of Truth,
     2007), 66 [With modernised terms].

In the entire work of salvation in Christ, 'nothing is introduced that derives from humans. It is God's work totally and exclusively; it is pure grace and undeserved salvation.'[6] This starts with the promise of salvation made by the whole Trinity. Election is the outworking of this. First Christ is chosen as Saviour, and then the Elect are chosen unconditionally, by the will of a loving God (Rom. 9:11-12). And we are always and only chosen in Christ (Eph. 1:4). As theologian Robert Letham reminds us, salvation is a person – the Lord Jesus. 'The entire plan of salvation, from the purposes of God in eternity to its outworking in human history, comes to focus in Jesus of Nazareth.'[7]

Now we turn to the arrival and devastation of sin through our parents Adam and Eve, anticipating the price for sin and the need for the Saviour to die.

---

6   Herman Bavinck, *Reformed Dogmatics III: Sin and Salvation in Christ* (Michigan: Grand Rapids, 2006), 229.

7   Robert Letham, *The Work of Christ* (Nottingham: IVP, 1993), 56.

QUESTIONS

IN ANCIENT DAYS: *ELECTION*

The Father's electing love is only ever 'in Christ Jesus'.

1.   Why is it so vital to understand that believers are elected *in* Christ?

2.   In what ways do Christians confirm their election (2 Pet. 1:10)? How can you personally strive in this from day to day?

3.   Read 1 Thessalonians 1:4-5. What is the relationship between God's love and election?

4.   What spiritual comfort does the doctrine of election give to you?

5.   What is the destination of God's loving election?

Chapter 2

A Garden: Sin

For the wages of sin is death. (Rom. 6:23)

Of all places, sin started in a garden. Many of us know the story well. We can picture Adam and Eve, the garden, the trees, the serpent and the perfectly placed fig-leaves. We have seen them countless times in children's books. But we can bring these images closer to home. Imagine yourself in your own garden or favourite park. Picture yourself living there in full interaction with a great and loving God, enjoying a close creature-Creator relationship with Him. Imagine spending every day exploring His endless gifts of genius: husband, herds, and herbs; roses, rhinoceroses and river dolphins; galaxies, gibbons and grubs – everything excellent because a good and holy God made them. Perfection. Communion. Joy. Love. Worship. Freedom. Intimacy. Simplicity. Peace. Beauty. But then … temptation. You take what God hasn't given. You defy your Maker. Suddenly your garden sours: Rebellion. Shame. Guilt. Chaos. Anger. Blame. Judgement. There is a foul change as sin takes hold. And something new … stinking, rotting death.

THE ORIGIN OF SIN

Even *while* (or before as in our first chapter) humanity was rebelling against Him, God, in His grace, extended His mighty arm in salvation. 'God shows his love for us in that while we were still sinners, Christ died for us' (Rom. 5:8). This means we can look at the subject of our sin (or human depravity) with humility but also daring. In considering the Bible's teaching on sin it is important for us to acknowledge sin in our own hearts. Sin should never be studied as a concept detached from us. It is vile and deadly, and because of it the Son of God went to the cross. Spending time thinking about what sin is, and the urgency of the rescue mission, will refresh us with gospel clarity and worship for Christ the Saviour. We can glory in the fact that, if we are in Christ, 'there is no condemnation' (Rom. 8:1) and we have been 'set free from sin' (Rom. 6:7).

Enter: Sin

When God made Adam and Eve in His own image (Gen. 1:26) He graciously gave Himself to them to be their covenant God. He also gave them each other, for companionship in the covenant of marriage (Gen. 2:18). And He had given them a magnificent home – a world full of wondrous and beautiful things (Gen. 1:1-25). But they wanted more:

> Now the serpent was more crafty than any other beast of the field that the LORD God had made. He said to the woman, 'Did God actually say, "You shall not eat of any tree in the garden"?' And the woman said to the serpent, 'We may eat of the fruit of the trees in the garden, but God said, "You shall not eat of the fruit of the tree that is in the midst of the garden, neither shall you touch it, lest you die."' But the serpent said to the woman, 'You will not surely die. For God knows that when you eat of it your eyes will be opened, and you will be like God, knowing good and evil.' So when the woman saw that the tree was good for food, and that it was a delight to the eyes, and that the tree was to be desired to make one wise, she took of its fruit and ate, and she also gave some to her husband who was with her, and he ate (Gen. 3:1-6).

It is important for us to realise that this is no petty fruit dispute, like a child who helps themselves to the fruit bowl before dinner. Adam and Eve's sin could not have been more devastating. They actively and consciously disobeyed God. They were both completely culpable for their rebellion, having no right to plead innocent. We know from the book of Proverbs that 'the fear of the LORD is the beginning of knowledge' or wisdom (Prov. 1:7). This 'fear' is not a God-is-a-monster quake-in-your-boots kind, but a God-is-holy take-your-boots-off kind. It is awe, reverence and worship. Solomon is telling us that *the enthroning of God is the beginning of wisdom*. It is both ironic and telling that Eve and her husband Adam search for another type of wisdom, one that does not revere the Lord but self. Their rebellion against a loving holy God was not simply eating a shiny red apple. It was their conscious decision to pursue the *enthroning of themselves*.

This was their idolatrous *de*throning of God. Sure, Adam and Eve sinned with their physical appetite but pride and idolatry motivated their appetites. Are we not the same? Much of our own sin comes down to satisfying our appetites, but always there at the root of it all is pride and self. If the fear (or worship) of the Lord is the beginning of wisdom, then fear of man or self is the beginning of sin.

It's only just begun

Adam and Eve's disobedience was a rational decision made by two rational beings. Although they were tempted by Satan, they were fully responsible for their behaviour. Similarly, we can't excuse our sin with, 'It wasn't my fault!', 'I couldn't help it!', 'The devil made me do it!' Like Adam and Eve, we are tempted but sin is something we choose. And deplorably, we choose it every day.

This sparks questions on the origins of sin and evil. We know that neither can come from God. Our God is morally perfect; He is holy and sinless and hates sin (Lev. 11:44; Rom. 1:18). Because of His moral perfection it is logically impossible for Him to create evil or introduce it. Whilst Genesis 3 is explicit about the first sin, the Bible is pretty silent about the supernatural origins of sin and evil beyond this. We know sin and evil did exist before Eden because Satan arrives on the scene. But what *was* and *is* going on behind the scenes, with the revolt of Satan and his angels in heaven, is not developed.

What we do know is that Satan persuades Eve to do the very same thing he did. He lures her to usurp God's authority. The book of Jude verse 6 reveals the disobedience of some angels 'who did not stay within their own position of authority.' Paul refers to Satan's fall of pride in 1 Timothy chapter 3. Perhaps more significant however, are the words of Jesus in condemning some opposing Jews who had blasphemed against him. 'You are of your father the devil, and your will is to do your father's desires. He was a murderer from the beginning, and does not stand in the truth, because there is no truth in him. When he lies, he speaks out of his own character, for he is a liar and the father of lies' (John 8:44). The devil is a liar. Deception is his defining characteristic.

This deceiver is still active. He is defeated, but Peter still warns us to resist him (1 Pet. 5:8-9; cf. Jude 6). In Eden the devil was successful in coaxing humanity into sin. But the Holy Trinity did not delay in bringing salvation.

Breaking covenant

On our screens, in our books, newspapers and unfortunately in our families, adultery is a prevalent story. Stories of a wife or husband who, after a time of secret deliberation, made up their mind to faithlessly steer themselves into the arms of someone else. Adam and Eve made a similar catastrophic decision to break covenant with their Creator. They breached the bounds of promise and relationship that God had made with them and so their intimacy with God, and with each other, crumbled into nothing but a shadow of what it was. In reality they became enemies of God and pulled the whole of humanity down with them. Herman Bavinck writes that almost as soon as

> creatures came, pure and splendid, from the hand of their Maker, they were deprived of all their luster, and stood, corrupted and impure, before his holy face. Sin ruined the entire creation, converting its righteousness into guilt, its holiness into impurity, its glory into shame, its blessedness into misery, its harmony into disorder, and its light into darkness.[1]

---

1   Bavinck, *Dogmatics*, 3:28-29.

Sin entered, and guilt and shame came with it. Adam and Eve's once innocent nakedness now exposed their disgrace and vulnerability to judgement. Like the guilt-ridden adulteress hiding from her husband, they hid themselves from God (Gen. 3:7-8). A glorious garden of intimacy, worship and joy was now shrouded in blame. Adam blamed Eve and God, and Eve blamed the serpent (vv.12-13). How could there ever be reconciliation?

A swift promise: The protoevangelium

But we don't have to launch into this chapter without hope. Although humanity was thrown headlong into sin, we already know that salvation had been long planned. In Genesis 3, God's judgement came swiftly – He does not hesitate in cursing the serpent. Yet in the same breath He speaks of deliverance, 'I will put enmity between you and the woman, and between your offspring and her offspring; he shall bruise your head, and you shall bruise his heel' (Gen. 3:15). How gracious and merciful God is! Even as sin enters, the Lord speaks of the birth and victory of the Lord Jesus Christ. 'He shall bruise your head, and you shall bruise his heel.' These eleven words make up the protoevangelium, or 'first gospel', where God promises that a descendant of Eve – a man – shall crush the serpent's head. These words speak of Elected King Jesus buying back sinners through His death and resurrection. Paul uses echoes of this in Romans 16:20, 'The God of peace will soon crush Satan under your feet. The grace of the Lord Jesus Christ be with you.' Jesus Christ will undo what Satan has done. In the words of Derek Kidner, it is 'the first glimmer of the gospel.'[2]

---

2   Derek Kidner, *Genesis: An Introduction and Commentary* (Nottingham: IVP, 1967), 70.

Divine Initiative

Have you ever had an argument with someone and afterwards, during that tense time of distance and silence, wondered who was going to initiate making-up? Many of us know what it is to seethe away inside, defending ourselves. *I didn't do anything wrong! I don't need to apologise and I certainly won't be the first!* In our ugly pride we resent the task of beginning reconciliation and are slow to admit we were wrong.

Now imagine a quarrel where you are totally at fault (of course they never happen!). Your selfishness, and your selfishness alone, has broken an intimate relationship and you have wronged your loved one terribly. Suppose, however, that the expected menacing period of silence and blame is instead eaten up in an immediate declaration of love and desired restoration by the one you have offended. What grace! What love!

This is how God responded to our sin in Genesis 3:15. And we see it in the election and incarnation of Christ. Just as the estranged Father sped in passion to embrace his wayward, prodigal son (Luke 15:20); in love God ran to sinners through the sending of the Son who 'emptied himself, by taking the form of a servant, being born in the likeness of men' (Phil 2:7). We can be saved through union with the Son of God because He put on sweaty, grimy humanity. In the incarnation we see this divine initiative, 'our union with Christ is grounded on his union with us. We can be one with him because he made himself one with us. As always, the divine initiative comes first. Christ's union with us took place in his incarnation.'[3]

This divine initiative in the incarnation should make our hearts sing with awe and delight at God's love for us. The Almighty, Eternal God has sought to save you. He is the divine

---

3   Letham, *Christ*, 77.

lover and pursuer of *your* soul. In the incarnate Son setting His face upon the horrors of the cross, we see the jealous love of the Triune God who is faithful and steadfast to save His people from fatal rebellion (John 3:16).

Sin = death

Sin spread from a garden in Eden across the globe, in the hearts of men and women. It is a universal disease. You and I don't need to look far to see the mess of humanity. We are all infected. Scripture tells us, 'There is no distinction: for all have sinned and fall short of the glory of God' (Rom. 3:22-23). With the arrival of sin came a disturbing new development for humanity – death. And with this, an invention that the earth had not seen before – the grave.

In my youth I had a lot of different jobs. My very first job, at the age of fourteen, was washing up in the upstairs kitchen of a tearoom during the summer holidays. My second, a couple of years later, was a Saturday morning job of peeling and slicing onions at a local pizza place. The job didn't last long because the onions would make my eyes stream so badly, I could no longer see what I was slicing. After this I was a barmaid, a receptionist, a sales assistant, a check-out girl, a data-entry assistant, a barista, and a beach toilet cleaner, amongst other things. All these jobs I did for money – which was more of an incentive in some than others. I worked, undertaking what was required of me, in order to earn a wage.

The Bible tells us that 'the wages of sin is death' (Rom. 6:23). Have you ever thought about what this means? When we sin we earn something, just as in a job. We earn death. For just one sin we receive a fatal wage. Genesis 3 tells us that death exists because sin does. Adam and Eve were warned that if they succumbed and ate the forbidden fruit they would 'surely die' (Gen. 2:17).

Because of their disobedience, death – the fatal enemy – rules the world. 'Therefore, just as sin came into the world through one man, and death through sin, and so death spread to all men because all sinned' (Rom. 5:12).

WHAT IS SIN?

When we talk about sin we commonly think of sins we may commit: anger, deceit, greed, sexual immorality, gossip, drunkenness, and stealing, for example. However, we have seen from the Genesis story that at the heart of *all* our rebellion against God is pure idolatry – the desire to enthrone ourselves and not our Maker. We've all heard the saying, *What's at the middle of sin?* The answer is, of course, that pesky little 'i'.

Sin creeps around our heads and our hearts like a sneaky enemy waiting to pounce (Gen. 4:7). It is so subtle it even corrupts our good deeds. The book of Isaiah says 'we have all become like one who is unclean, and all our righteous deeds are like a polluted garment' (Isa. 64:6). The pride of Adam and Eve is so twisted throughout us too, sticking to every thought, word and deed, that even our acts of kindness are shot through with cunning and self-seeking. This is why it is so hard for our depraved, rebel hearts to recognise sin. Jeremiah hits the nail on the head, 'The heart is deceitful above all things, and desperately sick; who can understand it?' (Jer. 17:9).

The gift of the law

It is because of the treacherous nature of sin that the Lord God gave humanity a conscience. The conscience is a part of what theologians call 'the natural law'. This is much more than a friendly cricket named Jiminy whispering moral memes in our ear. This natural law means everyone is accountable: Jew and

Gentile. Paul speaks of this in Romans 2:14-15.[4] It is an integral law built inside all of us, giving us moral responsibility. John Calvin said that our human conscience is a God-given inner alarm bell that stops us from sleeping or resisting the debt we owe to God. Our conscience shows us the difference between good and evil and challenges us when we fail to do our duty. And yet, with all this, says Calvin, we are still 'wrapped in darkest ignorance'.[5]

To His special covenant people, the Lord God gave more than the natural conscience. After the Exodus out of Egypt, when God was making the people of Israel His own, He gave them the Ten Commandments (Exodus 20). Every commandment given springs from the very heart of a holy and righteous God, reflecting to this day, the moral perfection of God Himself. Every line of text etched into the stone was a grace; a boundary line to serve as a pair of moral glasses to discern God's holiness and their own unfaithfulness. The law was given to help them identify and acknowledge their sin. Now that they had it the people could compare the righteousness of God with their own. *Am I coveting what doesn't belong to me? Am I worshipping something or someone else other than the Lord? Am I being honest to others?* This is why the Westminster Larger Catechism says 'sin is any want of conformity unto, or transgression of, any law of God, given as a rule to the reasonable creature.'[6] Sin is, by definition, going outside of God's law, trespassing outside of it. It is a 'departure'

---

4   'For when Gentiles, who do not have the law, by nature do what the law requires, they are a law to themselves, even though they do not have the law. They show that the work of the law is written on their hearts, while their conscience also bears witness, and their conflicting thoughts accuse or even excuse them' (Rom. 2:14-15).

5   Calvin, *Institutes*, 109-110.

6   Westminster Larger Catechism 24.

from God's perfect law by a rational human race who know God's will.[7]

Now and then my family and I spend a week on Dartmoor in south-west England. The lodge is right in the middle of a large farm, with fields of grain, sheep and cows sprawling out from every direction. On the evening of our first visit, once the children were in bed, I decided to pull on my boots and do a reconnaissance of the area. After climbing over a gate or two, I soon found myself in a muddy field full of cows. Seeing a locked gate leading onto a lane on the other side – and wanting to do a clean loop – I headed towards it. However, when I got there, I discovered an electric wire strung from one side of the field to the other, blocking my way. I was sceptical. I couldn't hear any buzzing. And I was cross that a silly line of wire was hindering my evening stroll. After all, I wasn't a stupid cow and could jolly well climb over the gate if I wanted! Stubbornly, I put my foot on the bottom bar of the gate and pulled myself up. My shin grazed the line.

To say the shock was uncomfortable would be an understatement. Stunned, humbled, and a little shaken up, I retreated and trudged back home to wallow with a cup of tea. The farmer's rules came first. It was his farm and he could put an electric wire where he wanted. I had tried to trespass where I wasn't allowed to go. He had created a boundary marker to make my trespassing quite clear.

Contrary to the way many of us see it, when God gave the Israelites the Ten Commandments, He wasn't being judgemental, brutal or unloving. It wasn't a display of power to dominate and terrify. It had a purpose. He wanted to stun, humble, and shake up the people of Israel so that they could acknowledge their trespassing. God wanted to deal with Israel's sin so that

---

7   Bavinck, *Dogmatics*, 3:126.

He could live amongst them. Moses tenderly reassured the people at Sinai, 'Do not fear, for God has come to test you, that the fear [reverence] of him may be before you, that you may not sin' (Exod. 20:20). In giving them the law, the Lord was distinguishing His people from the rest of the world because He wanted to live in communion with them. He wanted to start restoring the intimacy of Eden. That's why, from Eden to Sinai to Calvary, God has been graciously dealing with sin. God's law reveals our desperate need for His mercy in Christ. A holy law from a holy God enables us to lose all delusions of self-righteousness. Knowing the extent of our weakness and sin means we can embrace Christ alone for righteousness and forgiveness.

What's so original about sin?

Original sin may seem like an awkward term in a world where 'originality' is used to describe the work of famous artists or a pair of designer jeans. Yet the Bible clearly teaches us that because Adam was the first human, and therefore the Father of the human race, Adam's sin corrupted the whole of humanity.

In recent years I have been easily convinced of humanity's original sin by the three gorgeous little things that live in my house. They are incredibly sweet and angelic looking, with wide blue eyes and blonde hair. But it wasn't long after each of their appearances – a year at most – that it became apparent that they *were* sinners. I remember well my first experience of this. My eldest had been nothing but adorable. But one day as a toddler she suddenly went berserk, screaming and fighting because I – so unreasonably – was trying to put her coat on. I was speechless at her irrational behaviour. *How could she be so naughty? What had happened to her? Was she possessed? Where could such behaviour come from? How could* my *child behave like that?*

And yet we shouldn't be surprised at all. After all it is *because* they are *our* children that they behave like this. Our sinfulness and irrational rebellion have been handed down to them – all because of Adam's sin in the garden. Man, woman, child – *all* have a fallen nature. All humanity (born or unborn) has a physical and natural solidarity under Adam. This makes him our representative, which we see worked out in the curses of Genesis 3:14-19. Because of Adam's rebellion he fell from immortality to mortality; from spiritual and physical perfection to spiritual and physical death.

But there is another Representative, a new Head that spiritually saves us. The second Adam – Jesus Christ.

Two giants

Picture two giants stomping along, both wearing giant belts. *Stomp, stomp, stomp!* This was the image that formed in Thomas Goodwin's (a Puritan theologian) head in understanding the spiritual representatives Adam and Christ. He saw Adam and Christ as having 'all the rest of the sons [and daughters] of men hanging at their girdle.'[8] You could say that these gigantic belts are lined with millions of hooks, and each human being either hangs off Adam's belt or off Christ's belt. This is a helpful illustration. We cannot be independent of these giants; we cannot avoid them. We are either on one or the other. Because Adam was the first human, we are all born onto his belt. Due to his rebellion in Eden we share in his fallen nature. But when we become a Christian something miraculous happens:

> When you received Jesus as your Saviour, you were involved in a massive and momentous transfer. The Almighty himself unhooked you from Adam's belt and hooked you on to Christ's.

---

8   Thomas Goodwin, *The Works of Thomas Goodwin* [Vol. IV] James Nichol Ed, 1862, 31.

> So you now have a different Head, a different Mediator, a new
> Representative ... You are in Christ unchangeably and for ever.[9]

This powerful, goose-bumps inducing doctrine is what
theologians call 'federal headship'. As Christians we are not
swaying utterly lost on the belt of Adam anymore! We are
connected to the Lord Jesus Christ – the second person of the
Holy Trinity. God's mighty gift of life in Christ 'is not like the
trespass. For if many died through one man's trespass, much
more have the grace of God and the free gift by the grace of that
one man Jesus Christ abounded for many' (Rom. 5:15). Adam's
sin is universal because of his headship. But thanks be to God,
this leads to the free gift of grace when we are transferred over
to the giant the Lord Jesus Christ.

Gross Consequences

Sin has cursed the world. We live on a planet perverted by sin
and groaning under the weight of it. Family breakdown, wars,
trolling, infertility, floods, cancer, terrorist attacks, and multiple
sclerosis, make up some of the junk pile of human suffering and
mess because of Adam and Eve's rebellion, as well as our own.
Sin has pushed and pulled our world into self-hate, disharmony,
decay and unpredictability.

The same is true for us as individuals. The power and
presence of sin from the inside and the outside has disfigured
us all. We are all marked with our own depravity and scarred by
other people's. The Westminster Confession of Faith describes
us as 'utterly indisposed, disabled, and made opposite to all

---

9   Edward Donnelly, *Heaven and Hell* (Edinburgh: Banner of Truth, 2001), 87.
     Gratitude to Rev. Donnelly for his visual development of Goodwin's metaphor
     which has been instrumental to my personal understanding and appreciation of
     union with Christ.

that is good', 'wholly inclined towards evil.'[10] This might sound outrageous to some of us.

Have you ever seen a photograph of yourself that has really shocked you? Because the camera has captured you from behind or from the side, and you are not used to seeing yourselves from that angle, you are suddenly hit with a dose of reality. If you are anything like me, you have seen such a photograph and cried out in repulsion, 'I don't look like that!', demanding some reassurance from your husband that the photograph doesn't resemble you at all. Unfortunately, my husband candidly answers every time, 'of course it looks like you. It's a picture of *you*!'

It is a little like this when we become a Christian and acknowledge our sin for the first time. The Holy Spirit shows us how vile we are. *Really? That's me? Yuck!* I love the way Augustine, the fifth-century theologian, shares his experience of this. He writes, the Holy Spirit took 'me from behind my back, where I had placed me, unwilling to observe myself; and [set] me before my face, that I might see how foul I was, how crooked and defiled, bespotted and ulcerous.'[11] Augustine writes in his *Confessions* that God did this 'that *I might find out my iniquity and hate it*. I had known it, but made as though I saw it not, winked at it, and forgot it.'[12]

How true it is that we wink at our sin! After all, we sin because we love it. Too many times we excuse sin as endearing habits, calling it 'cheeky' or charming in other people. Like teasing someone because they like to get up a bit of speed on the motorway or have an inclination for shopping sprees. Worse still is endearing sin to ourselves. In pride we offer a mock apology, 'Sorry, I just say it how it is!' or 'that's just who I am!' Augustine

---

10   The Westminster Confession of Faith 6 and Westminster Larger Catechism 25.

11   Augustine, *Confessions,* 8:7

12   *Ibid* [italics mine].

goes straight to the jugular of our sinfulness. God showed him his iniquity so he would hate it. We too must hate sin. It is not winsome and it is more than just irksome! Jesus went to the cross because of our sin. Whether it's breaking traffic laws, unhealthy spending, or speaking an unkind word, sin is offensive to our holy God. As we sing, it was our sin *'that held him there.'*[13]

Conclusion

The apostle Paul wrote that 'the wages of sin is death' (Rom. 6:23), meaning our sin earns us a place on Death Row. But 'God shows his love for us in that while we were still sinners, Christ died for us (Rom. 5:8). *Hallelujah!* As believers we are still full of sin, but we are not mastered by it anymore (Rom. 6:18). This is awesome news! Let's see how Jesus Christ bought us back from this slavery and made us His own.

---

13   Stuart Townend, 'How deep the Father's Love for Us.' 1995.

QUESTIONS

A GARDEN: *SIN*

'The cross stands as a memorial to the inexpressible horror of sin; it will not allow us to escape into self-deceiving optimism.'[14] But we are not hopeless. Jesus came to seek and save the lost. Sin has left us all in a great mess, but the one who came to take it is much greater.

1. How does God's promise of salvation in Genesis 3:15 change the way we see the whole of the Bible?

2. In what ways do we wink at sin?

3. Proverbs tells us that the fear (or worship) of the Lord is the beginning of wisdom (Prov. 1:7), and we said that the fear of man is the beginning of sin. How can this help us fight sin?

4. Read 1 John 1:8-10. What is our relationship with sin as Christians?

5. How do you know your sins are forgiven?

---

14   Steve Jeffery, Mike Ovey, and Andrew Sach, *Pierced for our Transgressions: Rediscovering the Glory of Penal Substitution* (Leicester: IVP, 2007), 159.

Chapter 3

A Cross: Death

... He made him to be sin who knew no sin. (2 Cor. 5:21)

At the end of the film *National Treasure*, after treasure seeker Ben Gates (Nicolas Cage) has been arrested for stealing the Declaration of Independence, Gates says to FBI agent Sadusky, 'I'd really love not to go to prison. I can't tell you how much I don't want to go to prison.' To which Sadusky plainly replies, 'Someone's got to go to prison, Ben.'

It's a rule of life, isn't it? Someone has to take the flack for the crime committed. The penalty must be paid by someone. In the same way, if 'the wages of sin is *death*' (Rom. 6:23), then *someone* has to die.

We have seen how sin reared its ugly and deadly head, cutting humanity off from intimacy with God. But the Holy Trinity had already planned to save men and women from sin's putrefaction and death sentence. *Salvation was to be executed by the execution of the incarnate Son – God made flesh.* 'For in him all the fullness of God was pleased to dwell, and through him to reconcile to himself all things, whether on earth or in heaven, making *peace by the blood of his cross*' (Col. 1:19-20). Paul's reference to blood here in Colossians is so important, and we shall see why throughout this chapter. The death penalty for sin has to be paid for by blood. Blood needs to be spilt. This is because life is in the blood. Leviticus tells us 'the life of the flesh is in the blood' and it is the 'blood that makes atonement by the life' (Lev. 17:11). This is echoed in Hebrews, 'without the shedding of blood there is no forgiveness of sins' (Heb. 9:22).

So how does Christ's blood have the power to save?

NOTHING BUT THE BLOOD

To understand the necessity of Christ's death to redeem us from sin, we need to go back to the significant yet foreboding night of the first Passover in Egypt. Due to the famine in Canaan, Jacob and his family settled in Egypt with Joseph. In his lifetime Jacob never returned to his homeland, only his bones made it back. Yet all the other Israelites stayed in Egypt (Gen. 50:14). Four hundred years later, this ethnic minority had become enslaved by their hosts (Exod. 1:8-11). But God had seen the oppression of Abraham's descendants and because of His covenant promises to Abraham and Jacob, He promised to set them free.[1] We join the story just after Egypt has endured bloody water, an onslaught of frogs, gnats, flies, boils, hail, locusts, utter darkness for three days, and the death of their livestock (Exod. 7-11). Pharaoh is stubborn; he still will not release Israel from slavery. So God tells Moses to instruct the people to take a lamb 'without blemish' and kill it at twilight on the fourteenth day of the first month, and use the blood to paint their doorposts and lintels (Exod. 12:5-7). God says in Exodus 12:13, 'The blood shall be a sign for you, on the houses where you are. And when I see the blood, I will pass over you, and no plague will befall you to destroy you.' The blood was a vital and saving sign because it pointed to and indicated the people's obedience to God.

And so it was: the angel of the Lord struck down in judgement those houses where there was no blood. Bare door posts and lintels – like gaping holes – screamed of the terror of death. Beloved sons, young or old, great or small, poor or rich, died that night. 'And there was a great cry in Egypt, for there was not a house where someone was not dead' (Ex.12:30).

If the blood of a spotless young lamb was dripping from the lintel, then God's judgement passed over that door, sparing the firstborn son because the lamb had died in his place. What a night! – as the dark terror of death crept around Egypt. Imagine yourself as a Hebrew woman preparing roast lamb, tension thick in the air, painfully aware that your husband and eldest son play together in the corner of the room. You follow Moses' instructions carefully, to make sure everyone wakes up in the morning.

---

1   See Genesis 12:1-7 and Exodus 6:5-7.

THE DOCTRINE OF SALVATION, FOR EVERY WOMAN

Jesus the Passover Lamb

After this horrific night the Passover meal was repeated every year on the first Jewish month, both as a sober reminder and a joyful celebration of the Lord saving Israel from judgement and slavery. Yet this annual celebration was blown apart centuries later in an upper room in Jerusalem, when God Incarnate declared Himself to be the ultimate Passover Lamb. We read in the gospel of Luke of the last supper between Jesus and His disciples, 'Then came the day of Unleavened Bread, on which the Passover lamb had to be sacrificed' (Luke 22:7). But have you ever noticed that no lamb is mentioned at the last supper? Jesus *is* the lamb.[2] 'And he took bread, and when he had given thanks, he broke it and gave it to them, saying, "This is my body, which is given for you. Do this in remembrance of me." And likewise, the cup after they had eaten, saying, "This cup that is poured out for you is the new covenant in my blood"' (Luke 22:19-20). The next day Jesus was killed. Except instead of a lintel His blood poured down a Roman cross. Paul testifies to this in 1 Corinthians 5:7, 'for Christ, our Passover lamb, has been sacrificed.'

This is why we sing about the blood of Jesus. To alien ears, Christian worship would sound gory and blood-thirsty.

> *Oh, to see the pain*
> *Written on Your face*
> *Bearing the awesome weight of sin;*
> *Every bitter thought,*
> *Every evil deed*
> *Crowning Your bloodstained brow*[3]

---

2   His 'references to his "body", and in particular his "blood … poured out", allude to his death, which he thus sets forth as the *decisive fulfilment* of the Passover festival.' Jeffery, Ovey, Sach, *Pierced*, 39 [emphasis mine].

3   Stuart Townend and Keith Getty, 'The Power of the Cross' 2005.

There is a fountain filled with blood,
Drawn from Immanuel's veins.
And sinners plunged beneath that flood
Lose all their guilty stains. [4]

What can wash away my sin?
Nothing but the blood of Jesus;
What can make me whole again?
Nothing but the blood of Jesus. [5]

Why would we want to rejoice in sharp thorns being pushed onto the thin skin of King Jesus' temple? Or the ruthless flogging of an innocent man? Surely Christians are pretty sick-headed to sing about His torturous death? But we joy in it because Christ's cruel death was a rescue plan, not an accident. It 'was the will of the LORD to crush him; he has put him to grief' (Isa. 53:10). The Father called His beloved Son to give Himself up as 'live-bait' rescue to a hateful, murderous crowd and carry His own means of execution up a hill to a place of sacrifice, to rescue us from drowning in our sin.

Mount Moriah

Many centuries before, another father had placed a heavy load of wood upon the shoulders of his only son, whom he adored. He was not a heavenly father however, but one who had waited with his wife through long years of infertility to have a child. When they finally conceived in old age it was nothing short of a God-given miracle (Gen. 21:1-2). This man and his son also slogged up a mountain because God had told the man to give up his son as an offering. The Lord had asked him to sacrifice the boy back to God, and the man obeyed. When his son asked his

---

4   William Cowper, 'There is a Fountain filled with Blood' 1772.

5   Robert Lowry, 'Nothing but the Blood of Jesus' 1876.

father where the lamb was to sacrifice, Abraham answered, 'God will provide for himself the lamb for a burnt offering, my son' (Gen. 22:8). Abraham knew God was in control. He continued to obey God's instructions and placed his son on the altar. Then a voice called to him to halt, 'Abraham, Abraham! ... Do not lay your hand on the boy or do anything to him, for now I know that you fear God, seeing you have not withheld your son, *your only son*, from me' (vv. 11-12). At the sound of bleating from a nearby thicket, Abraham found a ram and offered it to God in worship instead. This was not just an unlucky ram in the wrong place at the wrong time; God had provided a substitute for Abraham's son.

This unusual story of Isaac's redemption on Mount Moriah is a picture of Christ as our redemption on Mount Calvary. Abraham reflects the heavenly Father who truly did not spare His only Son as an offering (John 3:16). God Himself has provided the lamb.

In Our Place

How many times we have heard Christian speakers use sports substitution to illustrate Christ's saving death? In truth this is an abysmal illustration of Christ's salvation not least because biblical substitution is *penal* in nature. 'Penal' is a legal word for punishment. It is where we get our word 'penalty'. A penal substitute is quite simply someone, or something, taking a punishment in the place of the guilty. I remember as a child unkindly jumping into a lovely warm bath that my twin sister had poured for herself. Her loud shrieks broadcasted the injustice throughout the house, bringing my father upstairs. I was quickly removed from the bath and just as I was about to be physically reprimanded, my twin asked to be punished in my stead. It was pretty humbling to watch her receive the penalty for my offence against her – even for something so trivial.

The doctrine of penal substitution is the biblical teaching that, at the cross, Jesus Christ took the death, punishment and curse of sin upon Himself for fallen humanity. We know 'the wages of sin is death', yet Scripture tells us that Jesus took on that wage Himself. 'He made him to be sin who knew no sin, so that in him we might become the righteousness of God' (2 Cor. 5:21). God the Father placed all of our sin on the Son and punished Him in our place. This is a pretty radical doctrine. Recently it has become fashionable to deny this in the claim that it is too abusive for a loving and just God. But, as we have seen, it is not empty, selfish abuse but a sacrifice made willingly by God Himself for the forgiveness of sin. It is the reason the gospel is good news.

How about you? Has anyone ever taken the blame for something you have done? Did their selflessness surprise you, punching you deep in the stomach with humility and gratitude? In His great love, the Lord Jesus Christ went to the cross in order to clothe us sinners with Himself (this we will see later), destroying the power of sin that entangles us. So 'for the joy that was set before him [he] endured the cross, despising the shame, and is [now] seated at the right hand of the throne of God' (Heb. 12:2). How can we do anything but give Him everything?

THE DAY OF AT-ONE-MENT

With His people newly released from Egypt, God was ready for them to worship Him in righteousness. For this reason, at Sinai He gave Moses the Ten Commandments as a covenant gift; a wedding ring declaring Israel to be His Bride. Due to the people's lust for idolatry in forming the golden calf, the first two tablets shattered into pieces at the foot of the mountain (Exod. 32:19). And this breaking of the law only continued. It did not make the people righteous. Yet in the whole overarching redemption story in the Bible, this was the first serious step since Eden, towards restoration and reconciliation with God. We saw in our previous chapter that God's law was to help the people live in obedience and holiness towards Him. It wasn't given to sort the problem of sin out completely; it was never going to do that (Rom. 7:7, 13). The law exposes our sin; it doesn't get rid of it. The Ten Commandments are a God-given barometer for sin, outlining God's own righteousness and perfection still today. Without it the Israelites, and you and I, are blind to our mess.

The Lord gave more than this, however, bestowing on His people a temporary provision for forgiveness. To us the ceremonial laws may seem overly complicated and cultic. But they were given in love so that God could draw near to His beloved people. For many pages in the book of Leviticus we read of the different offerings the people could give in the tabernacle for particular sins (Lev. 1-7). These should amaze us. Our God thought of everything! His provision to the Israelites was generous and comprehensive.

The Day of Atonement is of particular importance. This special day of worship and sacrifice was set up by God to cover all sin, whether recognised or unrecognised. On only one day of the year (Heb. 9:7), the High Priest would enter a highly exclusive room behind a thick curtain – a heavy room divider that would one day be ripped from top to bottom (Matt. 27:51). Here, in obedience to God, the blood of goats and bulls was sprinkled so that God would forgive the people's sin. In this provision the Lord was 'merciful and gracious, slow to anger and abounding in steadfast love', offering forgiveness and not dealing with Israel as their sins deserved (Ps. 103:8-10). The Lord gave careful instructions for Aaron the High Priest to follow...

> Kill the goat of the sin offering that is for the people and bring its blood inside the veil and do with its blood as he did with the blood of the bull [Aaron's personal sacrifice for him and

his family], sprinkling it over the mercy seat and in front of the mercy seat. Thus he shall make atonement for the Holy Place, because of the uncleannesses of the people of Israel and because of their transgressions, all their sins ... For on this day shall atonement be made for you to cleanse you. You shall be clean before the LORD from all your sins (Lev. 16:15-16, 30).

These verses speak of blood washing the people from their uncleanness. Like you and me, the people were dirty and unclean in their sin. They needed to be washed otherwise God could not dwell amongst them. A holy and perfect God could have no intimacy with a people plastered in sin.

This reminds me of the condition of my three-year-old after certain meals. She can get so sticky. It's in her hair, on her clothes, smeared into her tiny pink fists and stuck between her fingers. It's everywhere. My husband and I hold her at arm's length until we can wash her. She is dirty and this brings distance, until she is bathed and smelling sweet in clean pyjamas. Then I hold her tightly next to me. I kiss her and get drooly kisses back. And my heart sings as she wraps her arms around my neck. She is clean. I do not hold her at arm's length anymore. There is at-one-ment again.

This is the vision. Christ washes us so that there can be complete and utter at-one-ment with His radiant spotless Bride, the church. This is the vision John has when he beholds a glorious army clad in pure white, washed by 'the blood of the Lamb' (Rev. 7:14).

Checking our theology

At this point your brow might furrow as you interject, *surely there is no power in the blood of animals to forgive sin! How can animals save God's people?* This is a good question and by it we can check our theology.

If the Day of Atonement and the whole of the Old Testament law truly saved then there would be no need for a second covenant in Christ (Heb. 8:7). The book of Hebrews tells us clearly that the offerings in the tabernacle, and later in the temple, 'can *never*, by the same sacrifices that are continually offered every year, make perfect those who draw near' (Heb. 10:1). This verse points us to Christ and His sufficient sacrifice. After all, every single year the High Priest had to revisit and re-atone. 'But in these sacrifices there is a reminder of sins every year. For it is impossible for the blood of bulls and goats to take away sins' (Heb. 10:3-4). The Lord Jesus Christ came, however, as the 'guarantor of a better covenant' that could save 'to the uttermost' (Heb. 7:22, 25). Christ, the Great High Priest, came and 'entered once for all into the holy places, not by means of the blood of goats and calves but by means of his own blood, thus securing an eternal redemption' (Heb. 9:12, 10:10-12). By the shedding of His blood on the cross, Christ 'put away sin' for good 'by the sacrifice of himself' (Heb. 9:26). The death of the Messiah restored God's people to Himself. Eden was undone. Sin's curse had been overpowered and reduced to nothing. And, as promised, Satan's head had finally been crushed by the offspring of Eve; Jesus of Nazareth, the Incarnate Son of God. Almighty God ripped the curtain of the Holy of Holies from top to bottom because the wage of death had been paid. Good Friday had become the new and real Day of Atonement. God had to rip that curtain up and *bring it down*. It didn't need to hang between humanity and God anymore because the Son of God was hanging on a tree a few miles away.

Blood Bought

You stand in rags and hefty bonds. Beaten, defeated and crushed, you can hardly lift your head. You are seduced by the very master who enslaves you. This Master Sin sneers and jeers at you, ready to pounce and demoralise you with empty promises and suffocating temptation. Yet you choose sin every time; overpowered in every word, thought and deed.

But there is grace. One man presents Himself in exchange for you. His very life; his blood spilled as a ransom, saves you from God's judgement (Mark 10:45). He dies a bloody and cruel death by spitters, mockers and murderers to buy your freedom. Making a fool of Sin, this man trounces death and walks away from the grave. The bonds that bound you drop to the dust and He escorts you out of Death Row into glorious light. Free from Sin's tyranny, robed in His righteousness, and now truly alive.

Salvation is a person

Augustine said that there are four crucial things to consider in every sacrifice: *To whom* it is offered, *by whom* it is offered, *what is* offered, and *for whom* it is offered.[6] We know that the sacrifice is offered *to* God because He is judge, the one who calls us to account. It was God that Adam and Eve disobeyed in the garden. Christ is the one *who* gives the offering because He is the perfect mediator between humanity and God. And we know that He offers Himself; His own life is *what* is offered. And lastly, we know that the sacrifice is offered *for* sinners who are lost in sin and hell-bound (John 3:16). Augustine applauds this salvation plan as perfect! That the sacrifice Himself 'might continue to be one with Him *to whom* He offered it, might be one with them *for whom* He offered it, and might Himself *be the offerer* and *what He offered*.'[7] Our salvation is truly a person.

---

6   Augustine, *De Trinitate* IV [emphasis mine].

7   *ibid* [emphasis mine].

Bearing sin

We have seen how, on the day of Atonement, the High Priest placed his hands on the animal and transferred the sin of the people onto its head (Lev. 16:21), so God the Father transferred the sins of the world onto Christ. This is why Paul writes, 'he made him to be sin who knew no sin' (2 Cor. 5:21). John tells us this is how the Lamb of God takes away the sin of the world (John 1:29). Christ's work is accomplished and need only then be applied to those who have faith (see Part Two). Isaiah foresaw King Jesus bearing this sin, 'He was pierced for our transgressions; he was crushed for our iniquities; upon him was the chastisement that brought us peace, and with his wounds we are healed' (Isa. 53:5). This isn't Christ suffering *alongside* His people. This is His deliberate self-sacrifice to be punished in the place of His people. There is no ambiguity, He is taking on their death sentence. 'He bore the sin of many, and makes intercession for the transgressors' (Isa. 53:12). Peter witnesses to Christ's fulfilment of Isaiah's words by echoing them. 'He himself bore our sins in his body on the tree, that we might die to sin and live to righteousness. By his wounds you have been healed' (1 Pet. 2:24). Have you ever realised that all the toxic and putrid mess of your heart was laid on Christ and crushed Him to death? Martin Luther powerfully explores this:

> According to the Law, every thief should have been hanged, therefore, according to the Law of Moses, Christ Himself should have been hanged; for he bore the person of a sinner and a thief – and not of one but of all sinners and thieves. For we are sinners and thieves, and therefore we are worthy of death and eternal damnation. But Christ took all our sins upon Himself, and for them He died on the cross. Therefore it was appropriate for Him to become a thief ... He is not acting in His own person now. [In one sense now] he is not the Son of

God, born of a virgin. But he is a sinner, who has and bears the sin of Paul, the former blasphemer, persecutor, and assaulter; of Peter, who denied Christ; of David, who was an adulterer and a murderer ... In short, He has and bears all the sins of all men [women and children] in his body ... He took these sins, committed by us, upon His own body.[8]

I am a thief. I deserve death. Jesus Christ was numbered with the thieves (Isa. 53:12) and became a thief for me. I am an idolater. I deserve death. Jesus Christ became an idolater for me. I am a murderer. I deserve death. But Christ bore my murderous thoughts for me. I am a liar. I deserve death. Jesus Christ became a liar for me.

It was now about the sixth hour, and there was darkness over the whole land until the ninth hour, while the sun's light failed. And the curtain of the temple was torn in two. Then Jesus, calling out with a loud voice, said, 'Father, into your hands I commit my spirit!' And having said this he breathed his last. Now when the centurion saw what had taken place, he praised God, saying, 'Certainly this man was innocent!' (Luke 23:44-47).

What an awesome redemption! If you are a believer you no longer deserve death. Your sins have been paid for in full. Perhaps you've felt pretty dismal looking at sin and the need for Christ's death. But we don't need to be discouraged. Instead we can dance for joy because the Lord Jesus has taken it all and set us free! Some of us harbour guilt for past sin. But the Son of God was publicly shamed, hanging naked on a cursed cross, for our shame. We are loved by God so much, that King Jesus gave Himself as an offering for our guilty souls (Isa. 53:10).

---

8   Luther's *Works*, Vol. 26 (Saint Louis: Concordia Publishing House, 1963), 277.

Understanding the Cross

The salvation of our God is neither modest nor simplistic. Redemption in Christ – in accomplishment and application – is as unfathomable as our Triune God. Depth and mystery abound. We might narrow salvation down to concise biblical statements (like the ever-famous John 3:16), which are true and helpful. But miles and miles of wondrous caverns and tunnels lie underneath to be explored by the willing mind.

It is true that the Lord has revealed this full and lavish salvation in His Word. What we find there can make our hearts burn with love and gratitude to our Saviour, if we take the time to study it. But we also need to appreciate mystery in understanding the cross. Scripture speaks about the cross with a rich tapestry of language and pictures, there is: ransom, reconciliation, propitiation, expiation, representation and substitution, that bring about cleansing, forgiveness, justification, redemption, satisfaction and victory. The same is true when we look at the person of Christ, and all His many titles. They work together to present Him biblically and truthfully. Similarly, one gospel theme on its own cannot tell 'the whole truth, nor do all of them together (at least as understood by us) exhaust the meaning of the cross. The various concepts are interrelated and inter-dependent, and together they give a thrilling and coherent picture of what the cross achieved.'[9]

It is a little like the movements of our planet. Many of us tell our children that the Earth rotates – spinning round and round, making life on Earth possible. Yet, there is more to it than this. The Earth does indeed spin on its axis, but its axis also 'precesses' so it looks like a spinning top about to fall. While we go round and round, the north pole is also making a slow

---

9   Donald MacLeod, *Christ Crucified: Understanding the Atonement* (Nottingham: IVP, 2014), 101-102.

circle meaning it is not always pointing in the same direction. If this was not enough, the Earth has another movement called nutation where the precession itself nods and wobbles with short-term irregularity. As these three movements pull away, the Earth is also orbiting the Sun once every year. These movements of rotation, precession, nutation and orbit are inter-related and inter-dependent in the life of the planet. We cannot correctly describe Earth's movement through space with just one of these four movements; they are all working together.

This is also true when understanding the biblical themes in the atonement. Like the inter-related and inter-dependent movements of the Earth working together, the biblical concepts or themes in the atonement all work together to produce salvation and life in Christ. The work of Christ on the cross cannot be appreciated fully if we only look at one part or if we just stick to familiar gospel verses. Therefore, before we finish, we must briefly consider two crucial 'movements' in Christ's work of atonement.

Diverting

Without Christ's blood we are, like the firstborn sons in Egypt, unprotected and exposed to God's wrath. Without His blood we are bare doorposts! The blood of Christ diverts God's wrath away from the sinner. The wrath of God is poured onto Christ instead of the believer. We saw in the Passover and the Day of Atonement something of this: the blood of the Passover lamb placated or appeased God, satisfying His judgement to the next door or for the next year. The blood of the spotless, sinless Lamb of God placates, satisfies and appeases the Father, saving sinners to God (1 Pet. 1:18-19). Paul uses the word 'propitiation' in Romans 3 to describe this diverting of God's wrath, 'God put forward [Christ] as a propitiation by his blood, to be received by faith' (Rom. 3:25). John uses the same word, 'In this is love, not that we have loved God but that he loved us and sent his Son to be the propitiation for our sins' (1 John 4:10). 'Now Christ made satisfaction, not by giving money or anything of the sort, but by bestowing what was of greatest price – Himself – for us. And therefore Christ's Passion is called our redemption.'[10]

Propitiation is appeasing an offended power. It is the pacifying or restoring of peace that was lost in Eden. When God the Father sees the Son's life blood and that the wages of sin have been met, His wrath is satisfied or diverted (Isa. 53:11). We must be careful, however, in considering this not to caricature God's wrath or divine anger. It is not unpredictable, proud and unkind like human anger. Instead it is a deliberate, proportionate and consistent response of a holy God to sin. And yet His wrath and His love are not at odds. Though utterly offended by our sin, the Father's love motivates Him to save. We don't read in the Bible, 'And because of his wrath, he sent his Son.' Instead, 'God shows his love for us in that while we were still sinners, Christ died for us' (Rom. 5:8). And 'For God so loved the world, that he gave his only Son, that whoever believes in him should not perish but have eternal life' (John 3:16).

We do not need to fear God's wrath. God loved us too much to leave us drowning. And He knows more than anyone that the price has been paid. 'Since, therefore, we have now been justified by his blood, much more shall we be saved by him from the wrath of God' (Rom. 5:9).

Covering

Thinking back again to the Day of Atonement where the blood was sprinkled upon the lid or 'mercy seat' of the Ark of the Covenant. The Old Testament word for this covering is where

---

10   Thomas Aquinas, *Summa Theologica*, III, q.48, a.4, ad 1.

we find 'expiation' or 'to expiate'. Interestingly, Hebrews speaks of Christ making 'atonement' or expiation for the sins of the people (Heb. 2:17, RSV). Here Christ's blood provides a covering from the wrath of God, removing the stain of sin by the washing of Christ's blood. Propitiation and expiation are closely related. '"Expiation" highlights the effects of the atonement on sin, whereas "propitiation" highlights its effect on God. Sin is expiated, God is propitiated.'[11] Propitiation, or the appeasing of God's anger at sin, is what Christ's death brought about, and expiation is how it happened. These are two essential inter-related and inter-dependent movements. We know they are essential because they are how the blood of Christ restores sinners to God.

Conclusion

On the 31st of October 1517, nail met wood and parchment as Martin Luther hammered 95 theses into the large door of All Saints' Church in Wittenberg. In these statements, Luther challenged the Roman Catholic Church, especially in the 'selling' of indulgences – a bizarre name for what was essentially a certificate declaring the purchaser to be forgiven. In reality they were spiritual knickknacks; utter junk! Nevertheless, men and women were putting their trust in these things and not Christ.

What do you put your trust in for forgiveness? Where do you look for salvation? Do you look to Christ or knickknacks … junk? Salvation is found only in the person of Jesus Christ. God has provided the blood of His Son for forgiveness and it is sufficient for you and me. What can save us from our sins? Nothing but the blood of Jesus.

---

11   Macleod, *Crucified*, 110.

Questions

A Cross: *Death*

Therefore, brothers [and sisters], since we have confidence to enter the holy places by the blood of Jesus, by the new and living way that he opened for us through the curtain, that is, through his flesh, and since we have a great priest over the house of God, let us draw near with a true heart in full assurance of faith (Heb. 10:19-22).

1. What does it mean that Christ 'knew no sin' (2 Cor. 5:21)? Why is this important to the gospel?

2. Use Scripture verses to demonstrate why it is so important that Jesus Christ is both God and man.

3. Why is Jesus the Great High Priest and what does this mean for our salvation?

4. What gospel truth in this chapter has specifically given you comfort?

   My sin — oh, the bliss of this glorious thought! —
   my sin, not the part but the whole,
   Is nailed to the cross, and I bear it no more,
   Praise the Lord, praise the Lord, Oh my soul![12]

5. Why do you think that the hymn writer used the word 'bliss' here?

6. What spiritual 'junk' do you find yourself trusting in?

---

12   Horatio G. Spafford, 'It is well with my Soul', 1873.

Chapter 4

An Empty Tomb: Resurrection

He is not here, but has risen. (Luke 24:6)

After His death Jesus' disciples buried Him inside a stone tomb because, for them at least, it was all over. We can read the gospel accounts in Matthew 27, Mark 15, Luke 23 and John 19. The grave was sealed with a large rock. BOOM! Never to be opened again … Or so they thought.

A couple of years ago my girls attended the funeral of their great-great aunt who had sadly passed away just months before her one hundredth birthday. At the burial, our eldest two scattered earth over the coffin and asked plenty of questions native to a four and five-year-old. My husband, who never likes to lose an opportunity to educate, explained that sometimes after a person dies, they are laid in a wooden box and placed at the bottom of a steep hole like the one before them. He told them the hole was to be filled with earth and the box would never be opened again. Understandably, the finality of this was hard for them to comprehend. They couldn't get their heads around the fact that Aunty Wendy was never going to wake up and get up again. It is this finality of death that many of us find difficult and painful to grasp. But we bury because of this finality. We seal the tomb because it *is* the end.

The Resurrection & the Life

It is our powerlessness to undo this cruel separation in death that moves us to violent grief when we lose someone we love. It was this loss in Mary of Bethany that moved the Lord Jesus to tears when Lazarus died. 'When Jesus saw her weeping, and the Jews who had come with her also weeping, he was deeply moved in his spirit and greatly troubled. And he said, "Where have you laid him?" They said to him, "Lord, come and see." Jesus wept' (John 11:33-35). King Jesus was not untouched by the devastation of human mortality. Here the promised offspring of Eve – soon to defeat death itself – mourns over the sting of the grave. However, only moments later He is declaring to Lazarus's sister Martha that He is Victor over death and Giver of life. 'Jesus said to her, "I am the resurrection and the life. Whoever believes in me, though he die, yet shall he live, and everyone who lives and believes in me shall never die"' (John 11:25-26). Then He, the divine Word made flesh, who spoke the universe into being (John 1:1-2, 14), calls the dead to life with the power of His voice. 'He cried out with a loud voice, "Lazarus, come out." The man who had died came out, his hands and feet bound with linen strips, and his face wrapped with a cloth' (John 11:43-44).

It was not long after this that Jesus proved the real extent of His power. By the power of the Holy Spirit, the great I AM, the Resurrection and the Life, deserted His own grave:

> Now on the first day of the week Mary Magdalene came to the tomb early, while it was still dark, and saw that the stone had been taken away from the tomb. So she ran and went to Simon Peter and the other disciple, the one whom Jesus loved, and said to them, 'They have taken the Lord out of the tomb, and we do not know where they have laid him.' So Peter went out with the other disciple, and they were going toward the tomb. Both of them were running together, but the other disciple outran Peter and reached the tomb first. And stooping to look in, he saw the linen cloths lying there, but he did not go in. Then Simon Peter came, following him, and went into the tomb. He saw the linen cloths lying there, and the face cloth, which had been on Jesus' head, not lying with the linen cloths but folded up in a place by itself (John 20:1-7).

I love Douglas Kelly's words 'the stone was rolled away from the door of the tomb, not to let the Lord out, but to let the disciples in, so that they could see that he was risen, and alive forevermore!'[1] Simon Peter and John saw the empty tomb and believed (John 20:8). Jesus of Nazareth had woken up and rolled the stone away. He had overpowered death and broken its neck.

---

1   Douglas F. Kelly, *Systematic Theology [Vol. 2]: The Beauty of Christ: A Trinitarian Vision* (Fearn, Ross-shire: Mentor, 2014), 461.

Prove it!

Have you ever thought what the state of affairs would be if it had been the end – if King Jesus had not risen from the grave? If this had been the case then He would still be lying in a sealed tomb in Palestine, powerless to save. You and I would be breathing with physical life but we would be dead spiritually, with no hope and no Saviour. Satan, sin and death would have conquered on Good Friday and we would still be hanging off Adam's belt dead in our sin, facing God's wrath and judgement. The gospel is good news precisely because the tomb is empty!

The Bible offers us evidence that the resurrection of Christ was a credible historical event. God sovereignly planned for a significant number of witnesses to see the resurrected Lord, and that this would be recorded in Scripture (Acts 1:3). Why else did the Lord Jesus appear to over 500 people after His death and some behind locked doors (1 Cor. 15:6, John 20:19)? Some people dismiss the resurrection as a farce pulled by Christ's disciples over the eyes of the Roman guards and leaders. But the post-resurrection scene in Jerusalem would have been very different had this been the case. It would have been anarchy. The disciples would have been arrested and the Christian faith would have lost all credibility. But instead, it spread like wildfire throughout the known world.

For those who have qualms about the proof of the resurrection, there are books that consider the biblical evidence for the resurrection clearly and logically.[2] This is important since there is no room in the Christian faith to accept the cross but deny the resurrection of Jesus. We can only run to the cross if we, like Peter and John, also examine the vacant tomb and linen cloths. This is because the resurrection is the climax of Christ's victory

---

2   See Josh McDowell's *Evidence for the Resurrection* and Lee Strobel's *A Case for Christ*.

against Satan. Albert Mohler says the empty tomb is the 'seal and confirmation' of Christ's person and His work of salvation.

> The resurrection of Jesus Christ has been under persistent attacks since the Apostolic age. Why? Because it is the central confirmation of Jesus' identity as the incarnate Son of God, and the ultimate sign of Christ's completed work of atonement, redemption, reconciliation, and salvation. Those who oppose Christ, whether first century religious leaders or twentieth century secularists, recognize the Resurrection as the vindication of Christ against His enemies.[3]

The death of Christ, therefore, cannot be separated from His resurrection. As Christians we must declare the Lord Jesus both crucified *and* risen – though sceptics frown and rationalists ridicule. For, as we shall see, there is no salvation in Christ apart from the resurrection.

A Risen Lord

Mary Magdalene and Mary (the mother of James) are lost and aimless in their grief. For them their teacher and Lord has been tragically murdered by jealous men. Yet as they walk to the grave, they meet a mighty angel. We know he was mighty because he says, 'Do not be afraid' (Matt. 28:5) – there is a very good reason why angels in the Bible always say this! The angel says, 'I know that you seek Jesus who was crucified. *He is not here, for he has risen*, as he said' (Matt. 28:5-6). Of course, Mary and Mary run off in great joy (v. 8). But then they meet Him. What did they do? … 'They came up and took hold of his feet and worshipped him' (Matt. 28:9). Women worshipping at the feet of the risen Christ … it is both sweet and awesome! We behold their worship in

---

3   Albert Mohler, 'The Empty Tomb and the Risen Christ – the Centrality of the Resurrection to the Christian Faith' (Online at www.albertmohler.com).

Scripture and what a vision it is for us. To simply see King Jesus, fall at His feet, and worship Him. Who could do otherwise? There is joy and there is worship because the Lord is risen!

Notice the angel says, 'He is not here, for he has risen, *as he said*.' He did say! He told them He would rise from the dead but the disciples missed it. John the Apostle remembers how early in Jesus' ministry, after He had stormed the local bureau de change and animal market out of the temple, He had said: 'destroy this temple, and in three days I will raise it up' (John 2:19). John writes in retrospect, 'he was speaking about the temple of his body. When therefore he was raised from the dead, his disciples remembered that he had said this, and they believed the Scripture and the word that Jesus had spoken' (John 2:21-22).

Resurrection Hope

If the stone had not been rolled away and the garden tomb had remained a place of sorrow instead of Easter celebration, there would be no gospel. This is why Paul wrote to the church family in Corinth, 'If the dead are not raised, not even Christ has been raised. *And if Christ has not been raised, your faith is futile and you are still in your sins*' (1 Cor. 15:16-17). We have no hope of future resurrection if Christ didn't trounce death. If Christ is still in the grave then we are doomed, still swaying dead in our sin off Adam's giant belt. The Christian faith hangs not just on a cross but on an empty grave. This is why the resurrection is vital! Christ's resurrection is not some happy, Disney tie-up at the end of a story. It is paramount to our salvation in Christ. It is imperative! The apostolic writers boast of the risen Lord throughout the New Testament; the resurrection is right at the centre of their salvation theology. It should be the same for us. Like Peter, we can't preach of Christ to others without powerfully proclaiming the resurrection (Acts 2:31-32). Like Paul, we can't write a letter or address our church without declaring Christ as risen; and we can't think upon our own death without trusting upon Christ's resurrection.[4] The resurrection is our creed and our confession. It is the reason behind our day of corporate worship, since the New Testament church moved the sabbath rest from a Saturday to the day of Resurrection. It governs our worship as we proclaim the Lord's death *until He comes* in taking the Lord's Supper (1 Cor. 11:26). The Lord is coming because He rose!

Pitiful Christians!

As a brand-new Christian in my early twenties, I spent a year doing church-based youth ministry. Now and then on a Friday my team would be involved in schools work; which meant leading R.E. classes and assemblies. On one visit to a senior school, after I had shared my testimony, a boy of twelve or so came up and asked, 'What if you are wrong? What if none of it is true?' I was flummoxed. I searched quickly through my brain for an answer and a Christian song lyric popped into my head:

> And if I die with no reward / Then I know I had peace cos I carried a sword.

I quickly quoted the line, trying to sound like some old sage. Although the boy nodded politely as he walked away, I knew he was as unconvinced as I was. The senselessness of my answer haunted me for a long time. And it wasn't until I stumbled over 1 Corinthians chapter 15 that I found the real answer to the boy's question, and it stunned me. *What if it's not true? What if we have it all wrong?* Paul says if Jesus Christ has not been raised then all preaching and all faith would be in vain, he would have lied about God, and the dead would have perished forever (1 Cor. 15:14-15, 18). It is verse 19 that is really shocking; 'If in Christ

---

4   Rom. 1:4, Gal. 1:1, Eph. 1:20, Phil. 3:10, Col. 1:18, 2:12, 3:1, 1 Thess. 1:10.

we have hope in this life only, we are of all people most to be pitied' (1 Cor. 15:19). Paul is not wavering but underlining the centrality of resurrection power in Christ.

I don't know what the writers of the song meant. It is difficult to make out their exact meaning. But if we do in fact die with no reward, if the Christian's hope in Christ fails at the end of this life, then we are of *all people* most to be pitied. *Of all people!* More pitiable than the most pitiable. Like those who die enslaved and denied any humanity. Or those who pass away alone and detested in their abuse of others. Or those who perish in anguish because they wasted their lives away. More than these? Our hope in Christ makes us empresses amongst beggars. If we, who thought we had a power beyond the grave, would in fact be left to maggot and mortality, how pathetic our end would be.

Of all the indictments against the Christian faith, it can never be called irrelevant – it boasts of victory over death. No one has ever avoided death in the history of the world! *But Christ!* Don't give me money. Don't give me fame. Don't give me beauty. These are all lost at the grave. Just give me Christ and His resurrection power!

United to Christ

Paul is teaching in 1 Corinthians chapter 15 that Christ's resurrection and our resurrection are not two different events but 'two episodes of the same event.'[5] The same divine power that raised Jesus from the grave also applies His resurrection to the Christian.[6] This means Christ's death is a *living reality* that can

---

5   Richard B. Gaffin, *The Centrality of the Resurrection: A Study in Paul's Soteriology* (Grand Rapids: Baker, 1993) 35.

6   Douglas Kelly stresses that the whole Trinity were agents of the resurrection. 'We see the entire Holy Trinity active in Christ's incarnation and in his atoning death, so we also see the Triune activity in his victorious resurrection. Hence, all that Christ was and continues to be for us as the one Mediator between God and

be applied to the believer through union with Christ. This is why Paul writes, 'I have been crucified with Christ. It is no longer I who live, but Christ who lives in me. And the life I now live in the flesh I live by faith in the Son of God' (Gal. 2:20). When we believe in Jesus the Holy Spirit takes our faith, joins us to our Saviour and makes His death our death. 'Do you not know that all of us who have been baptised into Christ Jesus were baptised into his death?' (Rom. 6:3).

This is true for His resurrection too. In our spiritual union with Christ we died but also walked out of the grave three days later, alive and victorious. 'For if we have been united with him in a death like his, we shall certainly be united with him in a resurrection like his' (Rom. 6:5). This is how the Triune God chose to save sinners, fusing His people to 'the Resurrection and the Life', making us alive together with Him in His death, burial and resurrection (Col. 2:12-13).

If the Holy Spirit does not apply Christ's death and resurrection to us by means of a spiritual union with Christ, then the saving work of Christ is like paint sitting in a tin and not applied to the wall. It is doing nothing! It only achieves its purposes once it is applied.

In our next chapter in part two we will begin to see that the gospel has everything to do with union with Christ.

Conclusion: Easter Victory!

We all know death has a real sting. Like a scorpion it delivers a quick, sharp and painful shock. In one instant, someone we love is gone. Many of us have buried a much loved one and our heart breaks for their loss. We would give anything and everything to hold them again. As Christian women we are united to

---

man is backed up to the fullest extent in the innermost life of the Triune God.' (Kelly, *Systematic*, 488-489).

the Resurrection and the Life. Our Lord Jesus Himself is our awesome comfort in the merciless face of death. He is the victor! 'O death, where is your victory? O death, where is your sting?' (1 Cor. 15:54-55).

A few years ago, my husband and I journeyed through a painful miscarriage. For three months we thought the pregnancy was fine. Like my other pregnancies I was pressing through morning sickness and could feel my belly growing. We had no reason to be concerned. But a scan on New Year's Eve showed a very different picture. The sac inside my womb was growing but our baby was not. We had lost our sweet one at around eight weeks. We were crushed. The pain of our loss seemed to hew large holes out of us. As fireworks and shouts of New Year celebration resounded all around me, I remember lying in the dark alone, waiting for my body to reject our precious child. Weeks later we buried our baby in the cold February ground. As snowdrops and daffodils heralded the hope of Easter, we found eternal hope in the powerful resurrection of King Jesus... And Easter came! Like Job, we were able to stand and say in our grief-ridden hearts, 'For I know my Redeemer lives, and at the last he will stand upon the earth. And after my skin has been thus destroyed, yet in my flesh I shall see God' (Job 19:25). Sin gave birth to the grave. Death came because of fallen humanity. But King Jesus lives! He was 'delivered up for our trespasses and raised for our justification' (Rom. 4:25). There are only victories on resurrection Sunday!

As we make the Easter victories of Jesus our anthem, we do not need to fear our own deaths. 'For since we believe that Jesus died and rose again, even so, through Jesus, God will bring with him those who have fallen asleep' (1 Thess. 4:14). We are one with Him who is the firstborn from the dead (Col. 1: 18). Samuel Rutherford wrote, 'Be not afraid, therefore, when ye come even to the black and swelling river of death to put in your foot and wade after him; the current, how strongsoever, cannot carry you down; the Son of God, his death and resurrection, are stepping-stones and a stay to you; set down your feet by faith upon these stones and go through as on dry land.'[7]

---

7   Rutherford, *Loveliness of Christ*, 74.

QUESTIONS

AN EMPTY TOMB: *RESURRECTION*

For the Lord himself will descend from heaven with a cry of command, with the voice of an archangel, and with the sound of the trumpet of God. And the dead in Christ will rise first. Then we who are alive, who are left, will be caught up together with them in the clouds to meet the Lord in the air, and so we will always be with the Lord (1 Thess. 4:16-18).

1. How did the women respond to the resurrection in Matthew 28:8-9?

2. Why is it so important to our Christian faith that Jesus rose from the dead?

3. Your non-Christian friend tells you the gospel is just a tragic story of an innocent man dying on a Roman cross. How do you respond?

4. Why did the resurrected Jesus appear to 500 or more people?

5. How should we, as women united to Christ, approach death?

PART TWO – SALVATION APPLIED

How God applies the saving death and resurrection of Christ to the believer

Chapter 5

A Spiritual Marriage: Union with Christ

Christ in you, the hope of glory. (Col. 1:27)

Where are you reading this book? Maybe you sit amongst Aspen-covered mountains in North America, or in a noisy coffee shop in Europe. Perhaps you are by peaceful turquoise shores or in dusty desert heat. No matter where you are, although Christ's death and resurrection took place on another continent from many of us, geography is irrelevant because of union with Christ.

It is the same with our place in time, since we were not living in the first century. Yet praise God, the Lord's accomplished saving work still rescues us, even though we live hundreds and hundreds of years later in an era saturated with blasphemy. The Saviour reaches us whether we are millennia or miles away because, when we believe upon the Lord Jesus, the Holy Spirit fuses us to Him. Without this oneness Christ's rescue mission is stuck in the past with no power. John Calvin puts it this way, 'As long as Christ remains outside of us, and we are separated from Him, all that He has suffered and done for the salvation of the human race remains useless and of no value to us.'[1] Therefore we have to be united to Jesus to be saved by Him.

You might have heard someone say that union with Christ is an important part of the gospel. But essentially union with Christ *is* the gospel. Indeed, the whole of redemption turns upon our oneness with Christ because it is the *process* of salvation as well as the *purpose*. John Murray agrees, 'Union with Christ is really the central truth of the whole doctrine of salvation not only in its application *but also in its once-for-all accomplishment in the finished work of Christ*.'[2] Murray goes on to say that the whole of salvation finds its origin in union with Christ. This doctrine is not about applying Christ's work retrospectively. Instead the Holy Spirit mysteriously united the elect with the crucified and resurrected Christ all those years ago.[3] So union with Christ is the method of salvation in Christ, as well as its goal.

This is exciting because it radically changes the way we understand not just the gospel, but the whole of our Christian lives. Christians are renowned for saying that their faith is all

---

1   John Calvin, *Institutes of the Christian Religion*. Trans. Ford Lewis Battles; ed. John T. McNeill (Philadelphia: Westminster Press, 1960), 3:1:1.

2   Murray, *Redemption*, 161 [emphasis mine].

3   *Ibid*, 162.

about having a relationship with Jesus. But the Bible doesn't teach this. The New Testament is crammed full of texts about believers being 'in Christ'. Should we then *base* our spiritual reality upon the undertaking of devotions, studies and programmes? Like a works-based spirituality? In fact, our relationship with Christ has been graciously given by means of a saving union with Him. The fact that Jesus unites Himself to us in order to save us means that the whole of our spiritual life is actually founded on this unbreakable, Holy Spirit-empowered reality. Every ounce of our practical spirituality should stem from our unity with Jesus, not on how 'spiritual' we feel from day to day. Therefore, this mighty and mysterious truth, which, as we will see, anchors the whole of salvation upon the person of Christ, is not just the basis of our salvation, but also our spirituality.

A Lavish Feast

Is it just me or are all-you-can-eat buffets not what they used to be? Those who have enjoyed a Nordic smorgasbord might agree that this is the all-you-can-eat *par excellence*. I remember beholding my first smorgasbord on a ferry trip to Norway as a child. The tables literally cascaded with elegant seafood, meat dishes, cheeses, breads and puddings. My sisters and I just stared at the food, our eyes as big as the hefty plates we held to our chests. We couldn't believe you could eat as much as you liked.

During a stay at a Colorado ranch some years later, I relived this luxury. We walked into the dining room on our first evening and the buffet was astounding! The cakes were literally stacked to the ceiling! We all tucked in whilst my father congratulated himself with the booking. After sating our hunger, however, we decided to pace ourselves. We were going to have an active week and didn't want to overstuff ourselves. Except, the next evening the decadent buffet didn't re-emerge. The lavish spread was only to welcome guests upon arrival. Disappointment was thick in the air as we slurped our way through cowboy casserole. We were undoubtedly not the first – nor the last – to experience such a bitter disappointment.

Salvation in Christ, however, is always generous and extravagant. It is a lavish banquet fit for a king ... yet offered to sinners (Luke 14:16-24). The Godhead spared no expense, and the very best – the Lord Jesus Christ Himself – is given without reserve. In Christ we 'eat what is good, and delight [ourselves] in rich food' (Isa. 55:2).

This unrestrained extravagance is displayed in the fullness of redemption application. *The 'application of redemption' is the term used by theologians for the great gospel gifts that are given by God to appropriate the accomplished death and resurrection in the life of the elect.* These gospel graces, such as calling, justification and glorification, are given by the power of the Holy Spirit. Paul speaks of some of them in Romans chapter 8, 'And those whom he predestined he also called, and those whom he called he also justified, and those whom he justified he also glorified' (Rom. 8:30). Here Paul connects one grace to another like links in a chain. This suggests that the application of *salvation in Christ is not one act but an unbreakable chain of gospel events.* Biblical theology also recognises faith, regeneration, conversion, adoption, perseverance, and sanctification as links in this gospel chain. All these together are the 'order of salvation' or the *ordo salutis.* Every event of grace is integrally joined to another; yet each is distinct with 'meaning, function, and purpose in the action and grace of God.'[4] This image of a chain is a neat unfolding of events worked by the Holy Spirit in the souls of men and women. This unfolding is at times either chronological or logical, as our coming chapters will demonstrate. Though there is some debate

---

4   *Ibid*, 80.

in theology over the sequence of these events of grace, this golden chain is a rewarding biblical tool for relishing the feast of salvation.

A Smorgasbord in Christ

When a person believes in Christ everything changes in a moment. We heard earlier from Calvin that while Christ is outside the sinner 'all that he has suffered and done ... remains useless'. But this is undone as the believer is fused into Christ *permanently*. Here the Christian becomes 'hidden with Christ' (Col. 3:3); gaining a new status or identity with new spiritual rights. She who was an enemy of God now enjoys a first-hand loving relationship with the whole Trinity (John 14:23, 26). Christ-bought redemption gifts are given: new life or regeneration (Eph. 2:5, Col. 2:13), justification (Gal. 2:17), pardon (Rom. 8:1, 1 Cor. 1:30), the continuing work of the Spirit in sanctification, and power in perseverance (1 Cor. 1:8, Phil.1:6, Jude 24). Unity with Jesus means adoption into God's intimate family, becoming a co-heir with Christ and the promise of a glorious inheritance (Eph.1:5, Rom. 8:15-17). One with the Saviour, the Christian is kept in Christ throughout life (John 6:39; Phil. 1:6), and given the certain hope of resurrection and glorification when the King returns (Rom. 8:11; 1 Cor. 1:2, 6:11; Rev. 14:13; 1 Cor. 15:22; Rom. 6:5-11; 1 Thess. 4:16-17).

None of us can hope to gain any of these spiritual joys and rights without faith in Christ. By faith, however, salvation is a smorgasbord *in* Christ. Paul is not exaggerating when he states that every 'spiritual blessing' is in Christ Jesus (Eph. 1:3).

WHAT IS UNION WITH CHRIST?

What does this union look like? How does God's Word characterise it? While the Bible is unapologetic in stressing the deep mystery of the believer's union with Christ (Eph. 5:31-32), it does speak of this union through illustrations, such as eating bread (John 6:26-58), a vine (John 15:1-16) a building (Eph. 2:19-22), a body (1 Cor. 12:12-27), and the marriage union between husband and wife (Eph. 5:22-35).

In John chapter 15 Jesus teaches His disciples about a spiritual unity they can enjoy with Him by looking at the parts of a grapevine. God the Father is the gardener who tends the vine, Christ is the vine itself, the central root and trunk, which precedes the fruit-bearing branches – which are believers (John 15:1-11). Here Jesus speaks of union with Him through the word 'abide'. 'Abide in me, and I in you. As the branch cannot bear fruit by itself, unless it abides in the vine, neither can you, unless you abide in me' (John 15:4). Frequently we read these well-known verses and suppose Jesus is speaking of communion with Himself. But if He were just referring to our relationship with Him then He wouldn't have spoken of this abiding in a *mutual* way. And yet He does in verse 4, 'Abide in me, *and I in you.*' So, we know this is to mean more than our devotional life, this is a shared oneness – a union: we are in Christ and He is in us. Jesus goes on to say that those who are one with Him are empowered to live fruitful lives of faith. 'I am the vine; you are the branches. Whoever abides in me and I in him, he it is that bears much fruit, for apart from me you can do nothing' (v. 5). Jesus is the organic, life-giving vine. Unless we are spiritually fused to Him, we are lifeless and lost.

Earlier in John we find Jesus teaching about saving union with Himself after His feeding of the five thousand (John 6:8-11). The people are still marvelling at His miraculous catering for five thousand plus people with the contents of a little boy's lunchbox. Jesus takes this opportunity to challenge them not to seek physical bread but spiritual bread. He powerfully tells them in front of the jealous religious leaders that *He* is the life-giving bread that comes down from heaven (John 6:33). 'Jesus said to them, "I am the bread of life; whoever comes to me shall not hunger, and whoever believes in me shall never thirst"' (John 6:35). Harking back to his conversation with the Samarian woman at a well two chapters before, where He describes himself as 'living water' (John 4:10), these great 'I AM' statements affirm His heavenly origin, ruffling the feathers of the zealous Jews (John 6:41). But Jesus goes a step further, controversially building on this analogy of Himself with bread by speaking of eating His flesh. 'I am the living bread that came down from heaven. If anyone eats of this bread, he will live forever. *And the bread that I will give for the life of the world is my flesh*' (John 6:51). The hard hearts of the Jews are not so much concerned with His musings towards cannibalism but the blasphemy and arrogance they hear. But here we find profound teaching about salvation in Christ. The Saviour is telling us plainly that we can only be saved by feeding on Him – His body and His blood – in faith.

> So Jesus said to them, 'Truly, truly, I say to you, unless you eat the flesh of the Son of Man and drink his blood, you have no life in you. Whoever feeds on my flesh and drinks my blood has eternal life, and I will raise him up on the last day. For my flesh is true food, and my blood is true drink. Whoever feeds on my flesh and drinks my blood abides in me, and I in him' (John 6:53-56).

Union with Christ couldn't be clearer in the passage; eternal, saving life is found only in the flesh and blood of God Incarnate. Robert Letham says of this mysterious teaching in John 6, 'As we eat, food becomes one with us. It enters our system, we digest it, and so we produce energy that enables us to live an active life. So, when we eat and drink Christ, he enters our system. He indwells us and, in turn, we remain in him. We grow into union … he in us his church, we in him.'[5]

This feeding on Christ through faith is integral to becoming a Christian, and we live this *spiritual* reality out *physically* as a church family in the Lord's Supper. Christ Himself gave us this sacrament as a tangible reminder and appropriation of union with His person (1 Cor. 11:23-29). In the bread and the wine, we do indeed spiritually eat in faith on Christ, enjoying full oneness with Him.

Bonded

Inside the medieval forge the blacksmith works to complete a sword by joining a blade to a hilt. He heats up the metals in the furnace and hammers the two objects into one desired whole. In eternity past, the fierce power of the Holy Spirit forges King Jesus to His elect and His elect to King Jesus. This forging is enduring, irrevocable, eternal. The Holy Spirit fuses Jesus to His Bride and Body, the church and His church to Him. He, the third person of the Godhead, is the power source that inseparably connects us to the Saviour (John 14:16-18). We cannot be connected unless the Spirit joins us to Him. He is the bond of union. 'You, however, are not in the flesh but in the Spirit, if in fact that Spirit of God dwells in you. Anyone who does not have the Spirit of Christ does not belong to him' (Rom. 8:9). How glorious that God Himself wraps us into Christ, hiding us safely in the cleft of the Rock that is King Jesus!

The union we enjoy with Christ is therefore spiritual, it is not a physical union like that of husband and wife. The power of our identity in Christ, however, does have physical relevance. Paul is forceful about this in his letter to the Corinthians.

---

5   Robert Letham, *The Lord's Supper: Eternal Word in Broken Bread* (Phillipsburg: P&R Publishing, 2001), 13-14.

Do you not know that your bodies are members of Christ? Shall
I then take the members of Christ and make them members of
a prostitute? Never! Or do you not know that he who is joined
to a prostitute becomes one body with her? For, as it is written,
'The two will become one flesh.' But he who is joined to the
Lord becomes one spirit with him (1 Cor. 6:15-17).

Our bodies belong to Christ because we are one with Him. We
are not our own, we 'were bought with a price' so as women
united to Christ we must 'glorify God in [our bodies]' (1 Cor.
6:20). This is an obvious place where our union with Christ
informs our physical lives. We must be sexually pure because we
are one with the perfect and beautiful Son of God.

Community

Whether it's the London-bred Mitchells, the somewhat creepy
Adams family, the yellow Simpsons, the vintage Cunninghams of
Happy Days – we love stories about families, don't we? Salvation
in Christ is actually a story of a family. We see this particularly
in our current doctrine due to the fact that union with Christ
is continually described as a community reality. Christ in union
with His Church, a body of believers, His corporate Bride. This
doctrine is closely related, as we saw in our first chapter, with
election. We cannot divorce union with Christ with this mighty
host who make up the elect. These are God's people, His chosen
ones.

Paul reminds the Christians in Corinth, Ephesus and
Colossae that they are joined to Christ who is the head of the
body, the church. None of us can miss how intimate and vital the
connection is between head and body – we depend on it every
day! The body is not only kept alive by the head, but grows, is
regulated, protected, controlled, fed, strengthened, equipped
by it. Just so with Christ who sustains the church, giving her

spiritual life and growth through an intimate and vital union (1 Cor. 12:12, 14-27, Eph. 4:15-16; Col. 1:18; 2:19). We must cling to Christ, 'holding fast' to him (Col. 2:19). Growing 'up in every way into him who is the head, into Christ, from whom the whole body, joined and held together by every joint with which it is equipped, when each part is working properly, makes the body grow' (Eph. 4:16). This also means the church family is one unified, physical body made up of different members. Therefore, Christians have a responsibility for their spiritual siblings because they are joined muscle, bone and sinew to one another in Christ. 'Here the Apostle encourages a covenantal sharing in one another's lives, a love and care for all the members of the Body that affirms the reality that the believer in Christ is covenantally one with his or her brothers and sisters in Christ.'[6] Similarly, Scripture teaches brothers and sisters in Christ are united together as a building, with Christ as the cornerstone.

> You are fellow citizens with the saints and members of the household of God, built on the foundation of the apostles and prophets, Christ Jesus himself being the cornerstone, in whom the whole structure, being joined together, grows into a holy temple in the Lord. In him you also are being built together into a dwelling place for God by the Spirit (Eph. 2:19-22).

Notice, Peter and Paul don't describe the household of God as a lean-to; we don't lean upon one another. We are *united* to one another as bricks fixed firmly together. Like a pile of unstable baked blocks is transformed into a home, so too a group of random individuals believing upon Christ become a living, breathing temple, joined together by Christ.

---

6   Natalie Brand, *Complementarian Spirituality: Reformed Women and Union with Christ* (Eugene: Wipf & Stock, 2013), 114.

That we share the mighty Christ belt with our brothers and sisters in Christ is a great gift. Many of us have issues with the church, suffering years of disappointment and pain through broken relationships. But in all its failures the church is the Body and Bride of Christ, greatly prized by Him and given for our sanctification and support. In a world of ever-shifting ideas on self, spirituality, belief and lifestyle – at the whim of society and media – Christians are in tremendous need of the stability of biblical doctrine taught *in* a biblical community. We must hold on to Christ the Head *and* the awesome covenant body with whom we have been knit together in shared union with Christ.

Sacred Wonder

All these parallels and metaphors teach us different characteristics of our union with Christ. Together they certainly reveal great truths of the 'in Christ' relationship, but they cannot, and do not, communicate it in its entirety. This sacred union is a mighty mountain of mystery that we cannot fully conquer or comprehend. As Paul exhorts his married readers to loving and self-sacrificial marriages he wrote of the mystery of the church being one flesh with Christ. '"Therefore a man shall leave his father and mother and hold fast to his wife, and the two shall become one flesh." *This mystery is profound, and I am saying that it refers to Christ and the church*' (Eph. 5:31-32). Paul is demanding a high view of marriage because it is an earthly reflection of the awesome prototype; the heavenly marriage between Christ and His church. But he is also underlining the profound mystery of union with Christ. Like many other God-truths, our finite minds are unable to cope with its majesty. Nevertheless, let's not shy away from this doctrine since we know that it fearsomely binds us to Christ. May it instead drive us to our knees in worship. 'On the glorious splendour of your majesty, and on your wondrous works, I will meditate' (Ps. 145:5).

Authentic Spirituality

Union with Christ is the key to a biblical understanding of the Christian life, putting the person and the work of Christ at the centre of *who* we are and *what* we do. Life in Christ is not some spiritual formula or equation, but a living, organic relationship that will last into eternity.

We are not saved by union with Christ and then left to our own devices. We grow by the Spirit into Christ, rooted in Him (Col. 2:6-7). Life can be impossibly hard but the spiritual union we enjoy with Jesus is profoundly relevant through physical, emotional or mental pain. Once we meditate on it we see that this Father-ordained, Holy Spirit-joined, intimate and permanent union with Christ is really our only source of comfort and security. This is why Paul questioned 'who shall separate us from the love of Christ? Shall tribulation, or distress, or persecution, or famine, or nakedness, or danger, or sword?' (Rom. 8:35). Not even death can prevail because He prevailed against it! 'For I am sure that neither death nor life, nor angels nor rulers, nor things present nor things to come, nor powers, nor height nor depth, nor anything else in all creation, will be able to separate us from the love of God in Christ Jesus our Lord' (Rom. 8:38-39).

The glory and wonder of saving union with Christ can impact every minute of every day, if we allow it. In years of loneliness or depression, in the devastation of finding porn on our husband's computer, or our teenager hurling fists and unrepeatable insults at us – in all of life's dark moments, we have this mighty, awesome reality and comfort. We are spiritually married to an all-sufficient Saviour in an unbreakable union. We have certainty and confidence; no one can yank us from Christ because God the

Spirit is the eternal bond. Sister, are you 'hidden with Christ in God' (Col. 3:3)?

Conclusion

Throughout the Old Testament we see the Lord pursue His people in steadfast love.[7] Whether Abraham in Ur, or Israel in Egypt, the desert, Canaan or Jerusalem, the Lord wants to dwell with His people. He wants the intimacy of Eden to be fully restored. He has waited since eternity for His chosen people, both Jew and Gentile, to be His own. The climatic fulfilment of this is union with Christ. First the eternal mysteries of the gospel began to stir into reality at the incarnation, as Yahweh finally meets His people through the Word made flesh (John 1:1-3, 14). But it is not until the Holy Spirit united the believer to the crucified and resurrected Son that *Immanuel* – God with us – is fully realised. Here the gospel is fully revealed, and 'the riches of the glory of this mystery, which is Christ in you, the hope of glory' (Col. 1:27). In union with Christ, the Triune Godhead buys back His people for Himself forever.

Christ's 'love hath neither brim nor bottom.'[8] When the Holy Spirit connects us to the Lord Jesus in faith, we are given endless mercies. Like a groom who gives everything he has to his bride, the Lord Jesus gives everything to His Bride the church. We are *called* to God in Christ, *made spiritually alive* in Christ for *faith* in Christ, *justified* by God in Christ, and *adopted* into God's intimate family in Christ. Our calling, regeneration, faith, justification and adoption are the goose-bumps truths of salvation applied. These doctrines make up the rest of this book.

---

7   2 Sam. 17:3; Isa. 62:5; Jer. 2:2; Ezek. 16; Hos. 1–14; Matt. 9:15; John 3:29; Rev. 19:7; 21:2, 9; 22:17.

8   Rutherford, *Loveliness of Christ*, 13.

Yet in all this, the best gift in salvation is the Saviour Himself. The Westminster Larger Catechism states that, 'The prime benefit of salvation is Christ himself. Salvation consists in union and communion with Christ.'[9] We are women who possess the greatest treasure – the Son of God is ours and we are His! What an extravagant rescue – as He enters the water to save us, King Jesus becomes our bridegroom and we His bride.

---

9   Robert Letham, *The Westminster Assembly: Reading its Theology in Historical Context* (Phillipsburg: P&R, 2009), 324-325.

QUESTIONS

A SPIRITUAL MARRIAGE: *UNION WITH CHRIST*

For you have died, and your life is hidden with Christ in God (Col. 3:3).

1. How can the glorious truth of union with Christ impact your life throughout the week?

2. When we are in the face of temptation, how can we fight our desire for sin with the truth of union with the Lord Jesus?

3. In what ways does shared union with Christ with your brothers and sisters in Christ challenge your view of church?

4. Augustine and John Calvin described Jesus to be incomplete without His church.[10] What do you think they meant?

5. What are the gospel graces that make up the order of redemption?

---

10 John Calvin, *Calvin's Commentaries: The Epistles of Paul to the Galatians, Ephesians, Philippians and Colossians.* Trans. T. H. L. Parker (Grand Rapids: Eerdmans, 1965), 138.

Chapter 6

Out of Darkness: Calling

He calls his own sheep by name. (John 10:3)

Voices chatting, birds singing, music playing, phones beeping, waves lapping, fire cracking, rain tapping, plates clattering … The audible life is all so familiar. Life is rarely silent. And in those scarce moments of still, still quiet, we always have the steady hum of the fridge. Life really is a barrage of noises.

The terms 'call', 'calling', or 'called' are used to describe addressing, summoning or even shouting out at someone. We 'call' to communicate, to get someone's attention, like a call to prayer or a wake-up call. When we talk about 'a call' we are talking about the audible.

God's call is not audible. Yet God's call, as it is taught in the Bible, is more overwhelming than the roar of an angry sea or an aeroplane flying right over your head. It is more life-changing than the first cry of your new-born baby. It is more intrusive than your 6am alarm. More comforting than the sound of the front door when you've been waiting up, worrying for hours. Far more exhilarating than the thump, thump, thump, of a concert so loud it resets your heartbeat. The spiritual call of the Most-High God to salvation is more powerful than anything in the audible life. It is the call 'out of darkness into his marvellous light' (1 Peter 2:9). You can't ignore it! The Lord said, when my word 'goes out from my mouth; it shall not return to me empty, but it shall accomplish that which I purpose, and shall succeed in the thing for which I sent it' (Isa. 55:11). God's call to His elect always achieves His purposes. This is why theologians use the term 'effectual call' to describe this drawing of God's elect to Himself. It is *effectual* or *effective* because it is an act of God 'and of God alone.'[1]

A Grand Invitation

Once there was a fine lady who hosted a great dinner party that put my Nordic Smorgasbord to shame. She spent months and months on the preparations, putting considerable thought into every detail. Motivated by sheer generosity towards her friends, she spent tens of thousands towards the most skilled chef and serving staff, an exquisite menu of seven courses, professional

---

1   Murray, *Redemption*, 89.

musicians, and elegant lighting and table-wear. Then she invited her friends with great expectation.

The day of the dinner party came and it was stunning. Exquisite flowers bedecked the rooms and calligraphed place-names awaited each honoured guest. But as the hostess eagerly waited, full of anticipation, text messages came flooding in with last minute cancellations: 'I'm in an urgent meeting with my estate agent' … 'I need to go pick up my new car' … 'We're on honeymoon.' Every excuse under the sun was made, and not one guest came. The decadent food began to grow cold. All the beauty was wasted. The hostess was appalled that all her guests had let her down.

This hostess had every reason to be cross, not least because her lavish invitation was to Buckingham Palace and she was the Queen. So, she sent her staff out to bring in the tourists and homeless off the streets of London … There was still room! She sent them out again, to drive in anyone they could find to fill the empty seats, so that none of her generosity was wasted.

I would think in actual fact, not many have declined the invitation of the Queen. But it helps us rethink a similar story that Jesus taught to demonstrate that although some are invited to the great feast of salvation, they do not come.

> At the time for the great banquet [the host] sent his servant to say to those who had been invited, 'Come, for everything is now ready.' But they all alike began to make excuses. The first said to him, 'I have bought a field, and I must go out and see it. Please excuse me.' And another said, 'I have bought five yoke of oxen, and I am going to examine them. Please excuse me.' And another said, 'I have married a wife, and therefore I cannot come.' (Luke 14:17-20).

This parable teaches us a necessary distinction when considering the call of God. The first invitation is the *external* preaching of the Word, the general call of the gospel to all. When Christians preach salvation, whether from the pulpit or over coffee, we fulfil the commission to share the good news of Christ. Like the man inviting his friends to his banquet, God uses this gospel proclamation to call out to everyone. However, many hear but reject the invitation to come. This is why Jesus quotes the prophet Isaiah to His disciples in Matthew chapter 13, 'You will indeed hear but never understand, and you will indeed see but never perceive' (Matt. 13:14, Isa. 6:9-10).

The second and third call to the poor and sinful is the *internal* and effectual call of God in the power of the Holy Spirit.

> Then the master of the house became angry and said to his servant, 'Go out quickly to the streets and lanes of the city, and bring in the poor and crippled and blind and lame.' And the servant said, 'Sir, what you have commanded has been done, and still there is room.' And the master said to the servant, 'Go out to the highways and hedges and compel people to come in, that my house may be filled' (Luke 14:21-23).

The parable illustrates that while many reject the common call of the gospel, some lost and needy sinners are effectually brought to the salvation-feast. Paul writes of this in his own preaching, 'we preach Christ crucified, a stumbling block to Jews and folly to Gentiles, but to *those who are called*, both Jews and Greek, Christ the power of God and the wisdom of God' (1 Cor. 1:23-24). Calvin reminds us this special 'call is dependent upon election and accordingly is solely a work of grace.'[2] That is why 'many are called, but *few are chosen*' (Matt. 22:14). This call is an act of God, it is 'holy' (2 Tim. 1:9), powerful, gracious and

---

2   *Institutes*, III.24.1

'heavenly' (Heb. 3:1). Because of God's divine power behind this summoning, rendering it always effective, this call of grace is irresistible to the human soul.

Chosen and Called

Election and effectual call are indispensably linked. Scripture tells us this, 'Those whom he predestined he also called' (Rom. 8:30). In the application of redemption, it is logical that God's call follows His electing love. If you are a captain of a sports team you first pick your players and then call out their names. This is done so they know they are chosen but more importantly to *activate* your choosing – to fulfil your purpose as captain. The team will only remain a dream in the captain's head unless the players are actually called out onto the pitch. God's election makes our calling intentional and intimate. When we choose someone, it is personal. That's why it hurts so much when no one calls our name out when teams are being called. We feel unloved and unwanted. But in His electing love, God does call us by name. His call is personal precisely because it 'is grounded in, or flows out of, God's sovereign elective purpose.'[3]

Although we are not able to express any experience of election, many of us can certainly articulate what it felt like when God drew us irresistibly from darkness into light. I remember for one disillusioned nineteen-year-old it started with the desire to stay at home and read her Bible, instead of going out with her housemate until the early hours. What looked at first like nostalgia for the safety of her Christian upbringing, took hold as a hunger for God and His truth. The call of God became tangible when I realised that a life spent in rebellion was not just ugly but utterly pointless. Here God called a sinner who was cold

---

3   Demarest, *Salvation*, 228.

towards Him and dead in trespasses (Eph. 2:1-10), by stirring up affections and need for Christ that had never existed before.

This powerful yet gracious call demonstrates God's sovereignty and initiation in salvation. He alone instigates. We cannot call ourselves just as we cannot elect ourselves, or regenerate, justify or save ourselves in any way. Nonetheless, this does not mean we do not respond; we still have to fully accept Christ. The Westminster Shorter Catechism states, 'Effectual calling is the work of God's Spirit, whereby, convincing us of our sin and misery, enlightening our minds in the knowledge of Christ, and renewing our wills, he does persuade and enable us to embrace Jesus Christ freely offered to us in the gospel.'[4] We are 'convinced' – not forced. We are 'enlightened' – not dominated. Our wills are 'renewed' – not overpowered. We are 'persuaded' – not controlled. We are 'enabled' – not suppressed. The Holy Spirit works in us so that our hearts and minds see the beauty and sufficiency of Christ for what it really is – *irresistible!* Murray says, 'The sovereignty and efficacy of the call do not relax human responsibility but rather ground and confirm that responsibility. The magnitude of the grace enhances the obligation.'[5] Although God calls, our wills still choose Him. And the Spirit makes it possible for us to do so as He changes our condition, giving us a new insatiable hunger, a God-given desire for Christ. In His grace, this cannot be quenched. None can resist His will (Rom. 9:19). Garry Williams writes that the sovereignty of God in calling us to Himself does not eliminate the 'human will and human action, but it does explain them. We are not to think that

---

4   Westminster Shorter Catechism 31.

5   Murray, *Redemption*, 92.

we make no choices, but that when we make choices we do so moved irresistibly by the Spirit of God.'[6]

The call of the holy Godhead may not be audible but it is more powerful than anything we can imagine. In it we have confidence: Spurgeon emphasised that if we sincerely desire God and His salvation then we can be certain we are under His call and will be accepted.[7] It is certain! For Christ said, 'All that the Father gives me *will* come to me' (John 6:37). If we, however 'find ourselves at home in the ungodliness, lust, and filth of this present world, it is because we have not been called effectually by God's grace.'[8]

What joy this doctrine is! In it we see the grace of the Father draw near to the sinner so that the sinner can draw near to God. 'No one can come to me unless the Father who sent me draws him' (John 6:44).

Called by our Father

A young father walks along the side of a river, his two-year-old daughter lags behind him, distracted with something. He stops, turns around and calls her name, instinctively calling her to himself. The little girl hears her name ... hears her father's voice. She looks up – the distraction forgotten – and grinning, runs into her father's loving arms.

When our heavenly Father calls us with power, by the Holy Spirit, He is calling us to Himself (Isa. 43:6-7). And He calls us by name. 'Fear not, for I have redeemed you; *I have called you by name, you are mine*' (Isa. 43:1). God isn't shouting to us in a blasé impersonal 'hey you!' manner. We will see in our next chapter

---

6   Gary J. Williams, *His Love Endures Forever: Reflections on the Immeasurable Love of God* (Wheaton: Crossway, 2016), 113.

7   Demarest, *Salvation*, 215.

8   Murray, *Redemption*, 92.

Jesus calling Lazarus out of the tomb by name, and so He does us. Calvin says we are being ushered into God Himself and His family, to be sons and daughters.[9] Joining God's family is always the destination.

This certainly redeems all those painful P.E. team selections at school. It also redeems a whole lot more. This mighty God-truth can heal the deepest of wounds. Have you been battered and ripped apart by those who were so supposed to love you most? Have you been left alone in divorce, abuse or absolute isolation; bleeding out any last bit of life and self-dignity? Listen to the voice of your Creator Father ... choosing you, calling you, loving you throughout eternity! In His Son He is calling you to Himself forever.

We shall see now why we need to be called by God; because we are dead. Completely and utterly lost and powerless. The call of God brings us into a place where we can be made alive. We need God to powerfully unhook us from Adam and transfer us to the belt of His Son Jesus Christ. We cannot shift ourselves; no amount of swinging and pulling is going to achieve that. 'For the mind that is set on the flesh is hostile to God, for it does not submit to God's law; indeed, *it cannot*' (Rom. 8:7). Only God has the power to change us. Perhaps, like me, you sat reading the Word of God in a dingy flat, and God called you out of rebellion. Or maybe you sat in a pew, listening to a sermon, and God drew you out of your tomb. Either way we cannot boast. We can only boast in Christ that God called us 'out of darkness into his marvellous light' (1 Pet. 2:9).

Conclusion

In the effectual call, those whom God chose in eternity are called by name into the glorious gospel graces of salvation

---

9   Calvin, *Institutes*, 484.

applied. Only those chosen 'in Christ' are called. John Frame writes, 'Note that in the application of redemption, each step intensifies our union with Christ. We are "in Christ" by virtue of our eternal election (Eph. 1:3), but by effectual calling we enter the "fellowship" of Christ (1 Cor. 1:9). The application of redemption draws us more and more deeply into Christ.'[10] The next gospel grace is that which we are called to, namely, new life with Christ.

10   John Frame, *Systematic Theology: An Introduction to Christian Doctrine* (Phillipsburg: P&R, 2013), 940.

QUESTIONS

OUT OF DARKNESS: *CALLING*

'Effectual calling summons us into all the blessings of salvation.'[11]

1. Read Acts 16:14-15. What do you think Luke means by 'the Lord opened her heart to pay attention to what was said by Paul?' (v.14).

2. How is God's electing love related to His call?

3. In what way should God's divine call to salvation excite us to prayer for world missions and our own personal evangelism?

4. The Lord Jesus commissioned us to preach the gospel freely, always inviting people to Christ. When and where do you have opportunity in your weekly commitments to do this?

5. How do James' words, 'draw near to God, and he will draw near to you' (Jas. 4:8) demonstrate our responsibility to come to God?

---

11   Frame, *Belief*, 939.

Chapter 7

From Death to Life: Regeneration

Therefore, if anyone is in Christ, he is a new creation.
The old has passed away; behold, the new has come.
(2 Cor. 5:17)

For a second after Aslan had breathed upon him the stone lion looked just the same. Then a tiny streak of gold began to run along his white marble back then it spread – then the colour seemed to lick all over him as the flame licks all over a bit of paper – then, while his hindquarters were still obviously stone, the lion shook his mane and all the heavy, stone folds rippled into living hair. Then he opened a great red mouth, warm and living, and gave a prodigious yawn … Everywhere the statues were coming to life. The courtyard looked no longer like a museum; it looked more like a zoo. Creatures were running after Aslan and dancing round him till he was almost hidden in the crowd. Instead of all that deadly white the courtyard was now a blaze of colours; glossy chestnut sides of centaurs, indigo horns of unicorns, dazzling plumage of birds, reddy-brown of foxes, dogs and satyrs, yellow stockings and crimson hoods of dwarfs; and the birch-girls in silver, and the beech-girls in fresh, transparent green, and the larch-girls in green so bright that it was almost yellow. And instead of the deadly silence the whole place rang with the sound of happy roarings, brayings, yelpings, barkings, squealings, cooings, neighings, stampings, shouts, hurrahs, songs and laughter.[1]

Stone-dead

As those born into sin, we are stone-dead. We have no spiritual life in us. Dead in Adam, our hearts are hard and 'uncircumcised' (Col. 2:13, Eph. 2:1). Yet the Lord promises to give His stone-dead people hearts of flesh. 'And I will give you a new heart, and a new spirit I will put within you. And I will remove the heart of stone from your flesh and give you a heart of flesh. *And I will put my Spirit within you*, and cause you to walk in my statutes and be careful to obey my rules' (Ezk. 36:26-27). These verses speak of a heart transplant for rebellious Israel but they also herald the regenerating work of the Holy Spirit in salvation. The promise 'I will put my Spirit within you' is the awesome indwelling of the third person of the Trinity. Jesus announces this before He goes to Calvary, 'I will ask the Father, and he will give you another Helper, to be with you forever, even the Spirit of truth,

---

1   C. S. Lewis, *The Lion, the Witch and the Wardrobe* (London: Harper Collins, 1990), 152-153.

whom the world cannot receive, because it neither sees him nor knows him. You know him, *for he dwells with you and will be in you'* (John 14:16-17).

In order for saving faith to take hold, the Spirit must come upon the chosen and the called and breathe spiritual life upon them. This new life then gives way to faith. Without it the sinner is still dead and unresponsive to the things of God. When Holy Spirit life flicks through the sinner for the first time, there is warmth, colour, activity, joy and worship! Like the breath of Aslan, this breath of God transforms ugly, cold death into beautiful life. *Regeneration is God's Holy Spirit undertaking open heart surgery, giving to His beloved elect a new heart that is malleable and responsive to His breath of life.* This is the gospel grace of regeneration, 'When the goodness and loving kindness of God our Saviour appeared, he saved us, not because of works done by us in righteousness, but according to his own mercy, *by the washing of regeneration and renewal of the Holy Spirit'* (Titus 3:4-5). It is as though we are in the water, inert like a corpse, indifferent to the danger we are in. Then the Spirit generates new life in us so we awake and suddenly see our dire situation. The gift of faith is then the realisation and will to cling onto Christ as He wraps Himself around us and brings us into His safety. Without the Holy Spirit's life-giving power, we have no spiritual muscle to cling to the Saviour.

WHAT IS REGENERATION?

Nicodemus was a man who needed spiritual life. He was completely in the dark about salvation. Except he was a Pharisee, a member of the Sanhedrin, and a scholar of Hebrew law, religion and politics. If anyone should have known about God's salvation it would be Nicodemus. But he was clueless ... literally. When Jesus gave him a hunch, Nicodemus missed it completely.

Nicodemus probably stood with the other Pharisees when Jesus was preaching. He, however, wanted to hear more. So he went to see Jesus in the same way I go for a run ... in the dark so no one can see! Nicodemus' first words are like the awkward approach of a desperate fan to a revered celebrity (John 3:2). But Jesus doesn't fuss around with pleasantries. He gets right to Nicodemus' spiritual state, telling him he won't see the kingdom of God unless he is 'born again' (John 3:3). In his response, Nicodemus' theology lands like a belly flop in the water, 'How can a man be born when he is old? Can he enter a second time into his mother's womb and be born?' (v. 4). It's almost too embarrassing to read. Nicodemus is way off!

Jesus sets him straight, 'Unless one is born of water and the Spirit, he cannot enter the kingdom of God' (v. 5). Though some traditions, particularly the Roman Catholics, think here He is referring to baptism, Jesus is speaking of a washing or cleansing from sin. Nicodemus would have understood this from the temple sacrifices. We see this also in Ezekiel chapter 36 before the promise of a new spirit. Ezekiel prophesies, 'I will sprinkle clean water on you, and you shall be clean from all your uncleannesses, and from all your idols I will cleanse you' (Ezek. 36:25). Water here is the cleansing work of regeneration by the Spirit. We have to be born again of water *and* the Spirit. This washing and new birth have to co-exist. As Murray says, 'Regeneration must cleanse from sin as well as recreate in righteousness.'[2]

Because of Nicodemus' 'mother's womb' *faux pas*, Jesus stresses that He is speaking of spiritual and not physical birth. 'That which is born of the flesh is flesh, and that which is born of the Spirit is spirit' (John 3:6). Jesus could not be plainer, this being 'born again' is of the Holy Spirit. He is the agent of it (Gal. 3:2-5) and consequently it is spiritual in nature. This is news for

---

2   Murray, *Redemption*, 98.

Nicodemus. The Lord Jesus is emphasising to this devout Jew that physical circumcision is meaningless for salvation. 'For neither circumcision counts for anything, nor uncircumcision, but a new creation' (Gal. 6:15). Nicodemus needs a heart transplant – *a circumcised heart*. Just as the Lord rebuked 'the house of Israel' who were circumcised in the flesh but 'uncircumcised in heart' (Jer. 9:25-26). Stephen too reproached the Jews who stoned him to death, 'You stiff-necked people, *uncircumcised in heart and ears, you always resist the Holy Spirit*' (Acts 7:51). We cannot resist the Holy Spirit. He alone can make us a new creation (2 Cor. 5:17).

We will see now how the Word of God, and the Lord in His conversation with Nicodemus, describes this new birth.

Mysterious and Secret

First Jesus teaches that regeneration is an *inward mysterious* work. The wind can do amazing things. It can work Arizonan sand into stunning waves of layered red rock, seas of rippled bronze sand in Namibia, great dunes in the Sahara, and seven-metre-high stone trees in Bolivia. The wind changes the surface of the earth, working constantly in power without being seen. Jesus says to Nicodemus in our passage, 'The wind blows where it wishes, and you hear its sound, but you do not know where it comes from or where it goes. So it is with everyone who is born of the Spirit' (John 3:8). This new birth is as mysterious as the wind. It is as mysterious as election and effectual calling. But it is real as the Holy Spirit is real, and we see this work in changed lives. R. C. Sproul says, 'The new birth is a mystery. And if it is a mystery to those of us who have experienced it, it is an impenetrable mystery at the fundamental level for those who have not experienced it – even for skilled theologians like Nicodemus.'[3]

---

3   R. C. Sproul, *What does it mean to be born again?* Crucial Questions no. 6 [Kindle Book].

The Spirit of God works *internally* in power in the souls of men, women and children. He works from the inside out. Not making someone socially acceptable for our middle-class church club, but moving sinners from death to life.

Immediate and Life Eternal

I love a good birthing story. It seems after giving birth many women want to share the trauma with those who can relate. Just the other day, I began chatting to a stranger in a coffee shop and within minutes she was telling me about the births of her children. We hear of long painful days. Disappointed expectations as the hospital sends labouring mums home. Labours that drag on for nearly a week. It's a big deal. Bringing forth a baby into the world takes time. The new birth of the Holy Spirit is *instant*, however. We know this because there is no middle ground; we are either born again or not. Unlike sanctification, which is the slow, progressive work of the Spirit making us holy. Regeneration is *immediate*. It cannot be slow, for this is a momentous exchange from Adam's belt to Christ's. Any delay would put us in danger. It must be done with speed.

Importantly, there are also no miscarriages or still-births in the Spirit's work of regeneration. The Spirit only brings about screaming, healthy spiritual life. 'You have been born again, not of perishable seed but of imperishable' (1 Pet 1:23). 'Regeneration is a work of the omnipotent power of God, power that nothing can overcome or resist. If God breathes a person back from the dead, that person comes back from the dead. There is no contest when this power is exercised.'[4] This life cannot be quenched. It is *eternal*. The Holy Spirit gives a spiritual life that extends into eternal life. It wasn't long after meeting Nicodemus that Jesus said, 'Truly, truly, I say to you, whoever hears my word

---

4   *Ibid.*

and believes him who sent me *has eternal life*. He does not come into judgement, but has passed *from death to life*' (John 5:24). The same power of God that raised Jesus from the grave resurrects us too into newness of life, and it is the same life that promises resurrection from the dead (Rom. 8:11). No matter how we are feeling spiritually the truth remains, if we belong to Christ, our spiritual veins are pumping with the Holy Spirit.

Faith in Christ is not a life-support machine that prolongs our lives in heaven once death steals us away from earth. Neither is it resuscitation. Salvation in Christ is God making dead sinners alive in Christ. 'And you, who were dead in your trespasses and the uncircumcision of your flesh, *God made alive* together with him, having forgiven us all our trespasses' (Col. 2:13). All the hooks on Adam's belt are hung with corpses. We must be transferred onto Christ in order to be made finally alive. Otherwise we remain enemies of God. Only God can make this mighty transfer from the doomed giant of destruction to the kingly giant of life and adoption.

CALLED TO LIFE!

Lazarus was dead. He had been dead for four days, sealed up in cloths and a cave. Lazarus could not fight death. For him it was well and truly over since he was powerless to stop his own demise and decay. Founded and fallen in Adam, Lazarus was utterly lost to sin and death. Nothing could save him.

Except the great I AM, the Resurrection and the Life (John 11:25), was walking as a man on the dusty earth towards him. He was coming! He was late, but He was on his way. Even as Lazarus lay cold and lifeless in the tomb, on the other side was one greater than death; the Word made flesh (John 1:1-5). And the Word *called*. 'He cried out with a loud voice, "Lazarus, come out!'" And at his words, breath entered the dead man. Life took hold at the power of his call. Lazarus was alive (John 11:43-44).

John Dick, a Scottish theologian says:

> the sinner is passive; for, till divine grace is exerted upon him, he is incapable of moral activity ... He is in the same situation with a man who is literally dead, and who, when lying in the grave, cannot contribute in any degree to the restoration of his life. He is like Lazarus, who had no concern in his own resurrection, knew not the voice which called upon him to come forth.[5]

The gospel grace of regeneration is free grace alone. It is not given because of any quality seen in us. Like Lazarus, we are altogether passive in it being given, as the Westminster Confession of Faith describes. The sinner can only answer the effectual call of God, and embrace the grace offered, once he has been 'quickened and renewed' by the Holy Spirit.[6] 'The believing and loving response which the calling requires is a moral and spiritual impossibility on the part of one who is dead in trespasses and sins.'[7] 'The natural person does not accept the things of the Spirit of God, for they are folly to him, and he is not able to understand them' (1 Cor. 2:14). This suggests that calling and regeneration overlap, and they do this so much that some theologians declare them to be the same process. These gospel graces are strongly synchronised and interrelated, though distinct. If regeneration did not occur together with the Father's call then it would be ineffectual and echo out returning to Him void. We know this never happens. But as God calls, He also brings to life! Through the Holy Spirit's miraculous, supernatural work we are given a new capacity. And

---

5   John Dick, *Lectures on Theology*, vol. III, 282. Cited from Kelly, *Systematic*, 480.

6   Westminster Confession of Faith 10.2.

7   Murray, *Redemption*, 95.

in the transformative power of the Spirit of life, we are set free in Christ Jesus from the law of sin and death (Rom. 8:2).

The grace of regeneration cannot and should not be separated from faith either. As we have said, new life must be given in order for faith to start burning in the believer. 'Without regeneration it is morally and spiritually impossible for a person to believe in Christ, but when a person is regenerated it is morally and spiritually impossible for that person not to believe.'[8] This means, as we shall see in our next chapter, that even our faith is a gracious gift from God.

Behold, the new …

Do you think Lazarus kept his grave clothes on after Jesus called him out of the tomb? Did he walk about in his smelly linen strips like an Egyptian Mummy or a zombie? I doubt it. Because he was alive his skin was glowing with life. He was no longer rotting. He would have taken off the old grave clothes, maybe burnt them, and put new fresh clothes on. 'Therefore, if anyone is in Christ, he is a new creation. The old has passed away; behold, *the new has come*' (2 Cor. 5:17). If you have called upon the Lord Jesus Christ to save you then you are a new creation. The old has gone. Therefore, clothes for the dead are not appropriate. Our new life in Christ means putting off our old grave clothes of sin and self, and clothing ourselves with Christ.

> Put to death therefore what is earthly in you: sexual immorality, impurity, passion, evil desire, and covetousness, which is idolatry. On account of these the wrath of God is coming. In these you too once walked, when you were living in them … seeing that you have *put off the old self* with its practices and have *put on the new self*, which is being renewed in knowledge after the image of its creator (Col. 3:5-7, 9-10).

---

8   *Ibid*, 106.

We must kill or 'put to death' (v.5) sin still present in us. Intentional violence against our pride, anger, lust, greed, selfishness, unfaithfulness, unkindness and all our evil, is proof of the Spirit's regenerating work in our hearts. At Calvary our sin received its death-wound. It has no place in us. John is forceful about this. 'No one born of God makes a practice of sinning, for God's seed abides in him, and he cannot keep on sinning because he has been born of God' (1 John 3:9). 'Cast away from you all the transgressions that you have committed, and make yourselves a new heart and a new spirit!' (Ezek. 18:31).

Conclusion

There is comfort in this mighty truth that we are *always* spiritually alive. When we have no appetite for reading Scripture and it feels as though only silence greets our prayers, we can know with certainty that we are alive in Christ no matter how dead we feel inside. Maybe at the moment you are stuck in a dry season and need some invigorating. Call upon the Lord for the Spirit of Christ to stir afresh His work of regeneration within you.

We are seeing more and more how the Holy Spirit applies Christ to the believer for salvation. This challenges our ignorance regarding the person of the Holy Spirit. Many contemporary Christians perceive the Spirit as the feel-good factor of Christianity, when the Father and the Son do all the hard work. This is blasphemy. Without the Spirit's work or 'operations' – as theologians call them – there would be no salvation in Christ. It is crucial to understand that 'whatever God in His grace works in us, it is *by the Spirit*.'[9]

In the Disney film *Moana,* the daughter of a Polynesian chief journeys across the ocean to restore a stolen heart. This lost

---

9   Arthur W. Pink, *The Holy Spirit* (Grand Rapids: Baker, 1978), 7 [emphasis mine].

heart is no ordinary heart but belongs to a living island called Te Fiti, and has the power to create and give life.

The end of the film has always struck me. With the lost heart, a pulsating green stone, in her hand, Moana looks for Te Fiti only to find a fiery lava monster standing in her way. But this *is* Te Fiti. Without her heart this beautiful living paradise is nothing but a vengeful monster of parched molten rock. Interestingly Moana tries to restore Te Fiti's heart to her but Te Fiti doesn't want to be saved; she only fights Moana with fireballs. Finally, Moana calls out to her through the smouldering fumes, and the black sooty monster relents and her heart is restored. Then a sudden and beautiful transformation takes place. Dusty lava rock transforms into a lush green paradise of flowers, palms, birds and plants. Darkness turns into light. Anger gives way to joy. And from death springs abundant life.

This is a powerful illustration of spiritual regeneration! Like Te Fiti we don't want to be saved. We don't even know we are lifeless and black, filthy with sin. But God calls out to us and darkness turns into light. Anger is burned up with joy. And luscious spiritual life takes hold. Radically and instantaneously, death is transformed into life.

Nothing brings joy like this new spiritual life. We can dance and sing. Praise God, we are no longer dead! We are alive, we are free!

QUESTIONS

FROM DEATH TO LIFE: *REGENERATION*

When the goodness and loving kindness of God our Saviour appeared, he saved us, not because of works done by us in righteousness, but according to his own mercy, *by the washing of regeneration and renewal of the Holy Spirit* (Titus 3:4-5).

1. What is regeneration?

2. What verses teach us that the Holy Spirit is the one who gives new life?

3. Why did Nicodemus struggle to understand what Jesus meant by 'being born again' (John 3:3-4)?

   Regeneration, faith, and conversion are not preparations that occur apart from Christ ... Rather, they are benefits that already flow from the covenant of grace, the mystical union, the granting of Christ's person.[10]

4. In your own words, what does Bavinck mean here?

5. Why is reading the Word of God so crucial to a life in step with the Spirit?

6. We all have loved ones whose hearts remain stone cold and dead towards God. Spend time praying that the Holy Spirit would move in their hearts and bring spiritual life in Christ.

---

10 Herman Bavinck, *Reformed Dogmatics IV: Holy Spirit, Church, and New Creation* (Grand Rapids: Baker, 2008), 525.

Chapter 8

Moving Mountains: Faith

By grace you have been saved through faith.
And this is not your own doing;
it is *the gift* of God. (Eph. 2:8)

Faith is a mountain mover. Faith is powerful stuff. Jesus taught that just a teensy amount can pick up a mountain and throw it into the sea. 'Truly, I say to you, whoever says to this mountain, "Be taken up and thrown into the sea," and does not doubt in his heart, but believes that what he says will come to pass, it will be done for him' (Mark 11:23). Faith is *so* powerful it can uproot a mighty mountain and toss it as though it were a pebble. Similarly, we read in the gospel of Matthew, 'If you have faith like a grain of mustard seed, you will say to this mountain, "Move from here to there," and it will move, and nothing will be impossible for you' (Matt. 17:20). Paul too understands this, 'If I have all faith, so as to remove mountains, but not have love, I am nothing' (1 Cor. 13:2). *Faith is a mountain mover.*

But what does this mountain mover look like in people's lives? We are told in the book of Hebrews that because of faith the believers of old – great heroes *of the faith* – lived Godward not earth-bound lives, trusting and believing against the tide of their families and communities, sometimes to the point of death. We know it was because of his faith that Abel offered God a sacrifice more acceptable than his brother (Heb. 11:4). And it was because of great faith that Enoch walked with God and did not die but was taken by God (Gen. 5:22-24, Heb. 11:5). By faith Noah constructed a giant boat – an Ark – although mocked by society; by faith Abraham left his home and followed God to a land of promise; and by faith Sarah was given the power to conceive at an old age (Heb. 11:7-11). Not forgetting Joseph, Moses, Rahab, all those who crossed the Red Sea and all those who obeyed and witnessed the fall of Jericho. Through their faith God moved seas and city walls … might as well have been mountains! And, as Scripture says, 'And what more shall I say? For time would fail me to tell of Gideon, Barak, Samson, Jephthah, of David and Samuel and the prophets' (Heb. 11:32). These all 'died *in faith*' (Heb. 11:13), and their faith changed everything. And yet 'the faith that shook down the walls of Jericho, the faith that raised the dead, the faith that stopped the mouths of lions, *was not greater than that of a poor sinner who dares to trust the blood and righteousness of Jesus Christ when he is in the jaws of all his sins.*'[1]

---

1   C. H. Spurgeon, *Faith* (Whitaker House, 1995), 20-21 [emphasis mine].

In this chapter we are going to see *what* faith is and *why* it is impossible to be saved without it. We will also consider that moment we come to Christ, that 'initial human response to the Spirit's working in the heart'[2] commonly known as conversion, and how to fight when our faith falters.

WHAT IS FAITH?

True spiritual faith is not the same as blind faith – that irrational hope that something exists although you can't see it. Contrary to George Lucas' leap of faith in *Indiana Jones and the Last Crusade* (1989), believing is not shutting your eyes and stepping out over an infinite abyss in the hope that something firm will meet your foot. Hebrews tells us that 'faith is the assurance of things hoped for, *the conviction of things not seen*' (Heb. 11:1). Essentially, this conviction centres on Christ; it is the certainty of the grace of God and His saving mercy readily available to us in Jesus. It is vital that Christ is the object of our faith because faith that is not focused on some*thing* or some*one* reliable is blind and irrational. Preacher Charles Spurgeon asked, 'What is to be the object of my hope, belief, and confidence? The reply is simple: The object of faith for a sinner is Christ Jesus.'[3] Salvation is a person. B. B. Warfield says salvation is not found in faith as a sort of psychic act, 'The *saving power* of faith resides thus not in itself, but in the Almighty Saviour on whom it rests.'[4] Salvation centres on Jesus Christ, the 'author and perfecter of our faith' (Heb. 12:2, NASV).

---

2   Demarest, *Salvation*, 235.

3   Spurgeon, *Faith*, 11.

4   B. B. Warfield, *Biblical Doctrines* (Edinburgh: Banner of Truth, 1988), 504.

The Night the Jailhouse Rocked

In a Philippian jail we see faith take hold of someone who has only just tasted the saving power of Christ. Late into the night, whilst two missionary inmates are singing and praying (Acts 16:25), the salvation of gracious God penetrates a Gentile prison. Waking to a thundering earthquake that rocks open the prison doors, this sinner experiences an awesome need for Christ by the power of the Holy Spirit. 'And the jailer called for lights and rushed in, and trembling with fear he fell down before Paul and Silas. Then he brought them out and said, "Sirs, what must I do to be saved?" And they said, "Believe in the Lord Jesus, and you will be saved, you and your household"' (Acts 16:29-31).

Notice that the jailer cuts right to the chase and asks simply, 'what must I do to be saved?' His practical and candid question has the tone of a man who is dying to be rescued. And Paul's answer is equal to the question, 'believe in the Lord Jesus, and you will be saved' (v. 31). It is a straight question with a straight answer. Scottish theologian Donald Macleod rightly points out,

> Paul and Silas knew nothing of the jailer's past, nor of his inward spiritual condition. They didn't know whether he was convicted of sin, whether he was a seeker, whether he was born again or whether he was elect. Yet they confronted him at once with the imperative, 'Believe in the Lord Jesus Christ!' [5]

What happens next? The jailer believes and is baptised 'at once, he and all his family' (Acts 16:33). 'And he rejoiced along with his entire household that he had *believed* in God' (v. 34). The earnest faith of this jailer stands in stark contrast to the murderously cold hearts of many Jews whom Paul encounters in Acts.

---

5   Donald Macleod, *A Faith to Live By: Understanding Christian Doctrine* (Fearn: Christian Focus, 2010), 165.

What must I do? How can I be saved? By *believing* in the Lord Jesus. Paul wrote to the Ephesians, 'when you heard the word of truth, the gospel of your salvation, and *believed* in him, [you] were sealed with the promised Holy Spirit' (Eph. 1:13). 'If you confess with your mouth that Jesus is Lord and *believe* in your heart that God raised him from the dead, *you will be saved*' (Rom. 10:9). This believing in *Jesus* is more than a nod to His existence. We know that believing is 'trusting', 'having confidence in', 'being certain of', and 'to judge as right'. Yet faith 'is not believing *in* God', as R. C. Sproul says, 'it's believing *God*.'[6] Although this faith is a-ball-in-our-court, something we are commanded to do, it is a *gift* of God, 'a supernatural act, an effect produced by the power of the Spirit of grace … a persuasion of the truth concerning the Saviour.'[7] The Philippian jailer was a man clearly persuaded of Christ.

This biblical account demonstrates that when Jesus, God's given Saviour, is the object of our faith, our faith is a *saving* faith. The men and women outlined in Hebrews chapter 11 were saved by their faith in God and their faith was counted to them as righteousness (Rom. 4:22, Heb. 11:2,16). For us, on this side of the cross however, faith is *simply taking hold of Christ. Faith is a conscious response to God's grace in Christ.* We said at the beginning of this book that God's salvation in Christ is like a 'live-bait' water rescue, where the rescuer jumps into the water and takes hold of the drowning person. Faith is when we – the drowning – intentionally cling onto Jesus in the confidence that He will take us to shore. As we said, salvation is a person. We can only be saved when we are spiritually tied to the Lord Jesus Christ. Saving faith is *accepting Christ as our rescuer and resting upon Him alone for salvation.*

6   R. C. Sproul, *What is Faith?* Crucial Questions Series 8 [Kindle Book].

7   Arthur W. Pink, *The Holy Spirit* (Grand Rapids: Baker, 1978), 85.

This brings up another important characteristic of faith. As Christians we talk about 'accepting Christ'; this is because the gift of faith involves our wills. Although it is a work of God inside of us, faith is, by the grace of God, a *decision* of God's chosen to follow and love Christ. We shall see more of this later, but it is important for us to recognise that faith is an *active* decision for the believer. It is not passive nor robotic. We know this because when we worship, we are not passive or robotic. Just as we are willing and proactive in worship, we are willing and proactive in faith. Grace works persuasively in us and we behold Christ as God, Redeemer and King. We respond 'to the fact that He is "very God of very God" by bowing the knee in adoration and worship. Wherever there is such worship there is faith.'[8]

The Gift of Faith

Without Christ we are in a pitch-black dungeon sitting in the filth of our sin, and there is no light inside the dungeon or in us to help us see the reality of our situation. Only God can enlighten us. Can we believe on our own? How can we? As those hanging on Adam we are dead, we have no living eyes to see the beauty of Christ without God's help. We have no ears to hear the wonders of the gospel without the Spirit's grace. 'The basis on which a sinner comes to Christ is that he is dead, not that he knows he is dead; that he is lost, not that he knows he is lost.'[9]

Faith is not natural to our inclinations. It is not something we can conjure up. 'No one can say "Jesus is Lord" except in the Holy Spirit' (1 Cor. 12:3). Paul reminds the churches in Ephesians and Philippi of this, 'For by grace you have been saved through faith. And this is not your own doing; *it is the gift of God*' (Eph. 2:8). '*For it has been granted to you that for the sake of Christ you should*

---

8   Macleod, *Faith*, 168.

9   Spurgeon, *Faith*, 32

not only believe in him but also suffer for his sake' (Phil. 1:29). A woman dead in sin has no capacity to call upon the Lord. Just as it was impossible for Lazarus to call himself out of the grave. A dead person cannot talk, cannot desire, cannot see his own blackness. But 'what is impossible with man is possible with God' (Luke 18:27). And through God's gift of faith mountains are moved, Everest is thrown into the sea and that which is lost and dead is made new. Nothing is impossible with faith because nothing is impossible with God.

The *Westminster Confession of Faith* calls faith 'a grace'.[10] When we appreciate our need for God to give us faith, we can understand fully the gospel; *it is all of God*. Salvation comes from the Lord truly and there is nothing of us in it. We bring nothing but our nothing, and God lavishes His grace on us.

> When we think about the riches of divine mercy by which we were redeemed and contemplate that even the faith by which we are saved came not from our own flesh and will, but as a direct result of supernatural intervention in our lives, we ought to be driven to our knees in gratitude and thanksgiving.[11]

As we have been exploring, it is one of the *many* gospel graces given to us by the Holy Spirit for salvation. In our first chapter we saw the dark, rebellion of our own hearts. We sensed something of the toxic stench of our sin and the mess we are in without Christ. And since we considered Christ's redemptive triumph in His death and resurrection, we have surveyed all the gospel graces that stem from this: The Father's electing love, our union with Christ, the divine call, the enlivening of our dead hearts, the bestowing of the gift of faith so we believe. And without this faith no gospel graces can follow. This would be the

---

10   Westminster Confession of Faith 14.

11   Sproul, *Faith*, 84.

end of the line. And yet because of all the mighty graces that came before, faith can only follow. The Word of the Lord always achieves its purposes (Isaiah 55:11). Justification and forgiveness of sin, adoption into the family of God, sanctification, holiness, preservation in life, and glory at the end are graces given because faith has taken hold of the Saviour. This is particularly important because it is faith that the Holy Spirit uses to unite us to Christ. We need faith for us to be connected to Jesus. Pink says, 'The principle bond of union between Christ and His people is the Holy Spirit; but as the union is mutual, something is necessary on our part to complete it, and this is faith.'[12] Without faith on our part, the Holy Spirit cannot fuse us spiritually to the Saviour because we are still unregenerate and dead in our sins.

Directive

Faith pleases God. In the gospels we even see Jesus numerous times marvelling at great faith (see Matt. 8:10, 9:2, 9:22, 15:28). When He meets the Centurion who has a paralysed servant, Jesus is enthralled by the faith of this Gentile, 'Truly, I tell you, with no one in Israel have I found such faith' (Matt. 8:10b). On the flip side, Jesus rebukes the 'little faith' of His disciples and the people (cf. Matt 6:30, 8:26, 14:31, 16:8, 17:20). Frustrated with their lack of faith He calls them a 'faithless and twisted generation' (Matt. 17:17). This is no surprise since we are told that 'without faith it is impossible to please [God], for whoever would draw near to God must believe that he exists and that he rewards those who seek him' (Heb. 11:6). Faith then is what God 'requires from us', it is a divine 'directive' for us.[13]

---

12   Pink, *Holy Spirit*, 85.

13   Macleod, *Faith*, 165.

Distortions

Many will disagree with much of this chapter, however. Particularly, with the biblical teaching that faith is a God-given grace for salvation in Christ. This, of course, is related to how serious your view of sin is, and how depraved you understand humanity to be. Some think that humanity has enough intrinsic good in them to believe and that we can work together with grace. Therefore, no immediate work of the Spirit is necessary. Instead, faith is the ultimate good work exercised by humanity. This theological position is not new but harks back to the teachings of Dutch theologian Jacobus Arminius (1560-1609).

Those who hold to a completely liberal theology will deny any need for grace at all. Usually when this is the case, Jesus Christ is not seen as Lord or Saviour, sin earns no judgement, and faith is just a more realised existence that appreciates the harmony between God and humanity. This waters down the glories of the gospel to a humanitarian philosophy, and no rescue mission is needed at all.

Scripture Soil

In a certain franchise of a particular Seattle-based coffee company in which I am sitting, one wall is nailed with big black letters, 'The quality of a good cup of coffee starts at the soil.' More than trendy wall art, this informs me that the rich flavour of my flat white is rooted in the rich soil in which the coffee plants grew. Quality soil equals quality coffee. This is true of faith. The quality of faith starts at the soil of Scripture. Theologian Herman Bavinck agrees, 'Just as a plant is bound up with the soil in which it is rooted and from which it draws its nourishment, so also the spiritual life is by virtue of its very nature bound up with

Scripture.'[14] Even the most hopeless gardener, of which I am the chief, can understand this. When replanting a newly bought plant it is tricky to separate the roots from the earth so you can spread the roots to be ready for a new home. They cling on so tightly, intertwined with the earth in which they grow. Strong faith is like this – it clings to Scripture; it grows in Scripture. It is strengthened and fed by Scripture. The more it intertwines itself with Scripture the more it grows in richness, depth and strength.

My faith is strong when my week is bound up in Scripture. But when I neglect the Word my faith suffers. I am always so surprised at how apparent this is; I never doubt when my face is in the Word. Sure, questions arise from what I am reading but my spiritual convictions are strong. When I let dust collect on my sword of the Spirit (Eph. 6:17), my faith is fickle and shakeable. Our faith is intertwined with the Word of God.

The book of Romans tells us that 'faith comes from hearing, and hearing through the word of Christ' (Rom. 10:17). This means the Holy Spirit uses the Word He inspired through the pens of the biblical writers to *illuminate* the elect to *faith*. This is why Paul urges Timothy to stay in the biblical truths, because 'from childhood you have been acquainted *with the sacred writings, which are able to make you wise for salvation through faith in Christ Jesus*' (2 Tim. 3:15). Scripture is the sword of the Spirit (Eph. 6:17), it is a weapon of truth authored by the Spirit of Christ. When the Word is read or preached it is like the Spirit rides on each word and powerfully works in hearts and minds. Spurgeon famously said, 'The Holy Ghost rides in the chariot of Scripture.'[15] The Word belongs to the Spirit and He uses it to wield faith. And faith flourishes from this majestic unity of Word and Spirit.

---

14   Bavinck, *Dogmatics*, 4:99.

15   C. H. Spurgeon. Sermon entitled, 'The Sword of the Spirit' (April 9th 1891).

Stressing the Bible in faith doesn't make conversion primarily intellectual. Biblically speaking, the emotional and relational features of faith must stay hand in hand with an intellectual acceptance of Christ and the truths of His gospel. Both aspects are needed. 'The new life implanted in regeneration yields, in relation to the intellect, faith and knowledge and wisdom; in relation to the will, conversion and repentance.'[16] We are not saved by our theological orthodoxy. The thief on the cross had a simple, saving faith. Yet when we embrace Christ, we also embrace the biblical confession of faith.

About-Turn!

Have you ever seen a military about-turn? Soldiers marching in unison, all in line, legs straight, chins up. All heading in the same direction. Then the sergeant bellows at the top of his lungs, 'ABOUT-TURN!' and suddenly, in a blink of an eye, everyone turns swiftly round and goes the opposite way.[17] The moment of faith in conversion is like this; it is an 'about-turn.' Living in death and rebellion, the Spirit grants us in an instant new life and faith in Christ. A new desire for Christ compels us to perform a 180-degree U-turn and we head the other way. From death → to eternal life. From judgement → to adoption. An enemy of Christ → we became His co-heir and He our brother. From love of sin → to hate for sin. From living in darkness → we run to the light. Standing in rebellion → we now bow in worship and repentance. 'Renewed by the regenerating grace of God, the believer is called to make *turning* from sin, dying to self, and striving to greater holiness a daily as well as a once-for-all

---

16   Bavinck, *Dogmatics*, 4:97.

17   This illustration is attributed to Rev. Bruce Jenkins.

matter. True conversion is a religious-ethical matter that involves the whole person in a *turn* from sin and to God.'[18]

When the gift of faith takes hold of us everything changes. How could we stay the same when faith and regeneration completely transform us? This moment of conversion, consists of repentance and faith by the sinner and is evidence of the regenerating work of the Spirit.[19] Conversion is the outworking or fruit of regeneration, which the New Testament uses the word repentance to describe (Mark 1:4). This transformation, as we will see in the next chapter, leads to the great transfer of our sin to Christ, and His righteousness to us, in the work of justification. But importantly it is faith that brings about this justification. Justification occurs only by faith; this justification brings peace with God. 'Therefore, since we have been justified by faith, we have peace with God through our Lord Jesus Christ' (Rom. 5:1).

Revolutionary Repentance

Some of the most revolutionary words from church history are those of Martin Luther in his first famous ninety-five theses, which he nailed to a church door in 1517, triggering the Reformation in Europe.

> When our Lord and Master Jesus Christ said, 'Repent' (Matt. 4:17), he willed the entire life of believers to be one of repentance.

These words shook the Roman Catholic Church to the very core; challenging much of its practice and power throughout the Continent. Rome had sold forgiveness in envelopes and supplanted repentance from the human heart and into the hands of a priest. Yet the moment of conversion hangs on our

---

18   Bavinck, *Dogmatics*, 4:97 [emphasis mine].

19   Demarest, *Salvation*, 290-291.

repentance. 'If God crushes us in godly sorrow, it is an act of sheer grace. It's His act of mercy to bring us to faith and conversion.'[20] If a sinner meets with faith in Christ, repentance has to burn in his or her heart. 'For godly grief produces a repentance that leads to salvation' (2 Cor. 7:10). The world nowadays also has little understanding of repentance. Not because of the heresy of Rome but because of the heresy of our hearts. Repentance is still revolutionary. And yet as those in union with Christ, we can repent boldly and with great confidence. Christ paid so dearly for us with His own blood and we are promised that 'there is no sin so great, that it can bring damnation upon those who truly repent.'[21]

When faith falters

You may not feel like your faith can move mountains. Perhaps you feel more like the disciple Peter sinking as overwhelming waves of doubt and uncertainty crash around you. Remember … your faith is a gift given to you by God. If you are a Christian then your faith has saved you and a mountain was moved when you were miraculously delivered 'from the domain of darkness and transferred … to the kingdom of his beloved Son' (Col. 1:13). Your faith is mighty because it is in a Mighty God.

So be encouraged, sister. Our faith can stand in the face of horrific suffering and persecution. Think of Darlene Deibler Rose who persevered for four years under false allegation in a Japanese Prisoner of War camp. Or young Felicity, who was arrested as a new believer, refusing to renounce Christ. Felicity faced wild animals in a Roman coliseum in Carthage in 203 AD, and after this – battered and bleeding – Felicity was killed by the sword. Or think about the missionary Helen Roseveare who

---

20   R. C. Sproul, *What is Repentance?* Crucial Questions No. 18 [Kindle Book].

21   Westminster Confession of Faith 15.

returned to the Congo for Christ, even after rape and kidnap. All these women had an 'assurance of things hoped for, the conviction of things not seen' (Heb. 11:1). They were normal women with God-given faith. You too can stand firm in such trials: in doubt, in uncertainty, in persecution, in loss, in pain, in loneliness, in spiritual confusion, and even in death.

> When I feel my faith will fail,
> Christ will hold me fast;
> When the tempter would prevail,
> he will hold me fast.
> I could never keep my hold
> Through life's fearful path;
> For my love is often cold;
> He must hold me fast.

As Christians, we all experience seasons when our faith falters. If this is you then cry out to God with the cry of the father whose son had a demon, 'I believe; help my unbelief!' (Mark 9:24). What a short yet profound prayer! If you are in union with Christ by faith, the power of the Holy Spirit works in you. Is your love for Christ cold and your heart distracted? Perhaps you are wilfully rebelling against a loving God? With faith draw near, remembering that though you falter, He will not.

> *Those He saves are His delight,*
> *Christ will hold me fast;*
> *Precious in his holy sight,*
> *He will hold me fast.*
> *He'll not let my soul be lost;*
> *His promises shall last;*
> *Bought by Him at such a cost,*
> *He will hold me fast.*[22]

22　'When I Fear My Faith Will Fail.' Ada Habershon (1861-1918)

Conclusion

Praise God for the simple grace of the gospel. Scripture tells us that 'Christ Jesus came into the world to save sinners' (1 Tim. 1:15). *Sinners!* Not the humble Church-goer, the earnest seeker, not the self-sacrificial church warden or ministry wife. Not the dynamic preacher or the astute theologian. Not the passionate worship leader or the generous entrepreneur … Christ came to save *sinners!* 'Every man as a man', every woman as a woman, 'every sinner as a sinner, the foulest, the vilest, the most vicious'[23] is welcome at the foot of the cross. This is the gospel.

We have seen that faith does not lean on some goodness within us. All of salvation depends on the goodness and grace of our God, and we only bring nothing except our need. We have faith in God because He is *faithful* to save. The Word of God tells us, 'If we confess our sins, he is faithful and just to forgive us our sins and to cleanse us from all unrighteousness' (1 John 1:9). May we then, tremble in fear and awe, and as the Holy Spirit stirs faith in us wail, 'I must have Christ'. For saving faith cries, 'I must have Christ and Christ alone!'

---

23   Macleod, *Faith*, 170.

QUESTIONS

MOVING MOUNTAINS: *FAITH*

The life I now live in the flesh I live by faith in the Son of God, who loved me and gave himself for me (Gal. 2:20).

1.   What makes faith *authentic*?

2.   Why is understanding faith as a *gift* from God important to grasping the whole of salvation?

3.   What do you think it means to 'walk by faith, not by sight' (2 Cor. 5:7)? What does this look like in your own life?

4.   The author of Hebrews encourages us to 'draw near with a *true heart in full assurance of faith*' (Heb. 10:22). What does this mean?

5.   Why do you think prayer is frequently called the muscle of faith ?

6.   In what ways does reading the Word of God grow your faith and why?

Chapter 9

The Mighty Exchange: Justification

Jesus Christ the righteous. (1 John 2:1)

Have you ever thought about what freedom actually is and why it gives such joy? When incarcerated a person experiences the living death of the detention of their whole being. This imprisonment is not just geographical, the will is chained and with it the independence and distinctiveness that makes us all human. No creature was ever created for captivity, least of all humankind. God made us for freedom and our souls rejoice in it. When freedom is restored to one who has been caged like a bird, there is sudden boundless life, delight, prosperity, sweet liberation! In an instant a person can go from utter misery to absolute bliss.

One of the gospel graces that God bestows in salvation is justification. This is God the Mighty Judge declaring us righteous and free from condemnation in Christ. All of these prior grace events: election, union with Christ, the Father's divine calling, the Spirit's regeneration, and the gift of faith, move us towards this freedom (Gal. 5:13). Since our first chapter we have seen that in our sin we are doomed to darkness, death and judgement. There is no clemency or quarter in the taking of prisoners. The wages of death have been earnt and so, without Jesus, life is spent in the oppressive air of death row. But faith in Christ brings a beautiful day ... suddenly the wages change, the air is clear and we walk out of death row acquitted. Now the wages we enjoy are *eternal life*. Not because of our own righteousness but because of the righteousness of Jesus Christ. 'For all have sinned and fall short of the glory of God, and are *justified* by his grace as a gift, *through the redemption that is in Christ Jesus*' (Rom. 3:23-24). This means there is no condemnation, no blame, no sentence, no guilt. 'There is therefore now no condemnation for those who are in Christ Jesus. For the law of the Spirit of life *has set you free in Christ Jesus* from the law of sin and death' (Rom. 8:1-2). We are free! 'God holds us innocent.'[1] What a beautiful day! All because we have an *advocate*; Jesus Christ the righteous (1 John 2:1).

In this chapter we will be considering the doctrine of justification which involves the forgiveness of sins and a restored relationship with God. In this God-truth, we see Christ is the believer's vindication, defence, forgiveness, acquittal from death

---

1   Macleod, *Faith*, 152.

and judgement. *Justification is the declaration of our pardon, even innocence, founded on the saving work and person of Christ, whereby His righteousness becomes our righteousness.* Justification is a mighty mountain of joy in the Lord Jesus Christ.

We are going to briefly introduce this doctrine with three declarations: Free! Clean! Forgiven!

Free!

On the day you believed upon the Lord Jesus you gained a freedom in Christ that can never be robbed from you. God Himself has justified you so He will not and cannot condemn you. 'Who shall bring any charge against God's elect? *It is God who justifies*' (Rom. 8:33). And if God isn't going to condemn you, who can? What security and yet what freedom! 'Who is to condemn? Christ Jesus is the one who died – more than that, who was raised – who is at the right hand of God, who indeed is interceding for us' (Rom. 8:34). None can condemn those who are one with Christ, for He Himself is their Righteous and constant advocate and plea. Our justification is a person; Christ is our justification.

Clean!

With this freedom comes another pronouncement of Christ's merits or virtues over us. We know there is pride, skulduggery, greed and malice in our hearts, but because we are united to King Jesus we are declared with a loud and authoritative shout, 'CLEAN!' For believers are robed with their Saviour and the filth of their sin has been washed away. This is not an ethical statement: we still sin. It is a legal state. Our sin is blotted out from our account and we have no criminal record any more. The price has been paid; our clothes are clean. We are clothed with the garments of salvation and covered with a robe of righteousness (Isa. 61:10). There are no more stains.

Spurgeon once asked his congregation, 'You have seen the snow come down? How clear! How white! What could be whiter? Why, the Christian is whiter than that. When the blood-drop of Christ falls on him, he is white, "whiter than snow."'[2] By Christ's blood we are whiter than snow. 'Though your sins are like scarlet, they shall be as white as snow' (Isa. 1:18). Just as the leper approached Christ and begged Him, 'Lord, if you will you can make me clean.' The Lord will always respond to our repentance in the same way, 'I will, be clean!' (Luke 5:12). 'If we confess our sins, he is faithful and just to forgive us our sins and to cleanse us from *all* unrighteousness' (1 John 1:9). Christ is our righteousness.

Forgiven!

Gemma poked the foam on her coffee with a teaspoon and looked at her friend, her voice laced with desperation. 'The sermon on Sunday was great but I've been thinking about what was said about spiritual joy. It's not really something I have experienced. I feel too … guilty.'

Helen pulled her mouth into a sympathetic half-smile, 'What is it you feel guilty about?'

'I guess the relationship I had before I married Neil.' Gemma said, her eyes welling up a little. 'And how I spoke to my father in his last months. I used to get so impatient with him.' Gemma cocked her head to one side and ran a finger under her eye.

'Oh Gemma. Your sin has been forgiven. Removed as far as the East is from the West, remember?' Helen said.

'… I know. But what does that actually look like, Helen? I'm sick of this guilt. I want joy!'

---

2   *Ibid*, 52.

Many of us have been taunted by past sin for years, and our spiritual growth is hampered by this lingering guilt. This makes little sense since justification in Christ is not only God's declaration of 'FORGIVEN!' but the higher and greater announcement of 'INNOCENT!' The power of justification is knowing our sins are forgiven. Forgiveness and declaration of righteousness are simultaneous, logically they must happen at the same time. Because God's moral law has been met in Jesus Christ, borne in His perfect life and obedient atoning death (Rom. 5:18-19), there is divine satisfaction as the judge looks upon us but sees Christ. Like Gemma, we need to grasp the extent of Christ's atonement to buy our justification. Christ is our forgiveness.

WHAT IS JUSTIFICATION?

It is important we appreciate the significance of our justification in Christ. When we fail to grasp the power and victory of this gospel grace, we rob ourselves of a great joy unique to the Christian. Instead we carry around spiritual baggage like the rest of the world. Like the man who drags someone else's bag from the airport conveyor belt, sweating and struggling with it all around his visiting city before realising he only checked-in a carry-on. Christians still carry guilt and shame that doesn't belong to them but was given to Christ. This is devastating since this pardon and forgiveness in Christ is the heart of the gospel. Martin Luther was a man who understood this. He said, 'If the doctrine of justification is lost, the whole of Christian doctrine is lost ... if we lose the doctrine of justification, we lose simply everything.'[3]

Justification is the opposite of condemnation (Rom. 5:18). The Westminster Shorter Catechism tells us it 'is an act of

---

3   Luther's *Works*, Vol. 26 (Saint Louis: Concordia Publishing House, 1963), 9, 27.

God's free grace, wherein he pardons all our sins, and accepts us as righteous in his sight, only for the righteousness of Christ imputed to us, and received by faith alone.'[4] We know this righteousness in the believer is a *legal declaration* instead of an actual moral perfection because Scripture speaks of it in this way, using terms such as 'charging', 'record', 'debt' and 'counting' to represent this. For example, Romans chapter 4 says of Abraham, 'That is why his faith was "counted to him as righteousness." But the words "it was counted to him" were not written for his sake alone, but for ours also. It will be counted to us who believe in him who raised ... for our justification' (Rom. 4:22-25). This language is clear in Colossians, '[God] having forgiven us all our trespasses, by cancelling the record of debt that stood against us with its legal demands. This he set aside, nailing it to the cross' (Col.2:13-14). We see this throughout the whole of the Bible as the law of God must be satisfied. 'Justification is a judicial [or legal] act of God, in which He declares, on the basis of the righteousness of Jesus Christ, that all the claims of the law are satisfied with respect to the sinner.'[5]

A done deal!

Like regeneration, justification is *instantaneous*. You can't be made gradually free – you are either free or not. Again, this makes it distinct from sanctification. The declaration of our guiltlessness comes from *outside* of us: it comes from Christ. Whereas our sanctification is something that happens *inside* of us. Justification 'removes the guilt of sin', while sanctification 'removes the pollution of sin.'[6] This declaration of innocence in Christ is also once-for-all, past, present and future, because Jesus' sacrifice

---

4   Westminster Shorter Catechism 33 [emphasis mine].

5   L. Berkhof, *Systematic Theology* (London: Banner of Truth, 1969), 513.

6   *Ibid.*

is once-for-all, past, present and future. The offerings of the temple priests had to be reoffered, 'But when Christ had offered for all time a single sacrifice for sins, he sat down at the right hand of God' (Heb. 10:12). 'For Christ also suffered *once* for sins, the righteous for the unrighteous, that he might bring us to God' (1 Pet. 3:18). It is finished! A done deal! Your debt is paid and you are righteous in Christ. This means justification is a *complete exchange*. A debt can only be charged to one account. On the day of atonement, the people's guilt was given to the animal, so it couldn't be carried by the people as well. Your sin, shame, and guilt was placed on Christ. It cannot be on you as well. 'The transformation is complete; the exchange is positive and eternal … Your sins have sustained their death-blow, the robe of your righteousness has received its last thread. It is done, complete, perfect.'[7] There is no corruption in the court of God, you are free! You will never be guilty again.

By faith

Frequently we hear of 'justification by faith', emphasising the relationship between justification and faith. Justification can only follow faith, logically and chronologically, 'For through the Spirit, by faith, we ourselves eagerly wait for the hope of righteousness' (Gal. 5:5). Though we speak of 'justification by faith', this does not mean faith in-and-of-itself saves us. The language here can be confusing. Anthony Lane helps us, 'faith is effective not in itself but because it unites us to Christ. Justification is by faith alone not because of what faith merits or *achieves* but because of what it *receives*.'[8] Is faith the final and ultimate good work that saves us? No! Because faith is a gift to us, not something we earn.

---

7   Spurgeon, *Faith*, 51.

8   Anthony N. S. Lane, *Justification by Faith in Catholic-Protestant Dialogue: An Evangelical Assessment* (London: T & T Clark, 2002), 26.

In one way faith is the vehicle that drives us to Christ. Faith is *in Christ* and it is His accomplished redemption that saves us. Bavinck writes, 'we are on firm scriptural ground, however, when we tie justification to the death and resurrection of Christ. Our justification has been obtained by Christ; it is objectively accomplished.'[9]

Faith is not the ground of our salvation but the instrument that takes hold of Christ.

What are you wearing?

Since we are declared 'RIGHTEOUS!', we should ask what is righteousness? Righteousness is perfect purity, holiness, spotless, sinless, blameless, moral goodness, guiltless, faultless, untarnished, clean, innocence.

What are you wearing today? Take a look at your clothes ... Are you wearing the robe of Christ's righteousness or your own? Are you clothed with Christ? If you want to know what righteousness looks like – then look at Christ. In this mighty gospel grace Christ wraps us up in His robe of righteousness: all His obedience to the Father, all His kindness and love for His neighbour, all His honesty, all His blamelessness, all His sexual purity, all His clean thoughts and victory against temptation are given as we are united to Him. This is the righteousness we gain in salvation. Donald Macleod calls this the 'climax of justification: God's great, definitive statement as to what He thinks of us. We move from pardon to vindication; from deserving Hell to being of unblemished character.'[10] We will see now that there is nothing in us to deserve such a gift.

---

9   Bavinck, *Dogmatics*, 4:178.

10   Macleod, *Faith*, 153.

Nothing in Us

Israel is about to cross the Jordan. They have been wandering in the wilderness for forty years. Finally, they are going to enter their covenant inheritance: a rich land of 'brooks of water, of fountains and springs, flowing out in the valleys and hills, a land of wheat and barley, of vines and fig trees and pomegranates, a land of olive trees and honey' (Deut. 8:7-8). But Moses is concerned that the Israelites will soon forget that it is only by God's power that they will defeat the Anakim, a people far stronger than the Israelites. That it is because of God's covenant mercies that they are even still alive to receive this magnificent inheritance. Knowing their fickle pride, Moses warns them, 'Do not say in your heart, after the LORD your God has thrust them out before you, "It is because of my righteousness that the LORD has brought me in to possess this land" … Know, therefore, that the LORD your God is not giving you this good land to possess because of your righteousness, for you are a stubborn people' (Deut. 9:4,6). Moses then continues to remind them of all their rebellion and idolatry at Sinai.

This is a helpful reminder for us too. We are no different from Israel. You may sneer here, saying somewhat self-righteously, 'I am an Evangelical Christian! I don't believe in self-righteousness!' Nevertheless, the problem with human hearts is that religiosity and self-justification is our default mode. In reality the truth of justification by faith should cause our sanctimonious hearts to implode inside of us. But unfortunately, we slip back into old habits and forget too easily that there is nothing inside of us that can credit us to God. This is why we need the external or *alien* righteousness of Christ. No, I haven't moved into sci-fi. Theologians use the word 'alien' to underline that this righteousness is completely separate and outside of us. It is Christ's – you and I had nothing to do with it at all.

There is no righteousness in us to deserve the bounty of pardon, forgiveness, acceptance, freedom and acquittal in Christ; as well as all the other blessings of salvation. 'If you, O LORD, should mark iniquities, O LORD, who could stand?' (Ps. 130:3). Yet this lavish salvation is the best robe on our backs, the ring on our finger, shoes on our feet, the fattened calf, and the celebratory feast of the gracious father for his undeserving prodigal son (Luke 15: 22-23). None of this is given because of our personal works or even some worth inherently in us. It is all of grace.

No Freedom in Works

Over the gate to Auschwitz and a number of other Nazi concentration camps the words 'Arbeit macht frei' appears above your head. This means 'work sets you free'. It was, of course, a torment and a bitter irony that freedom would be promised in a place of profound human suffering and mass execution. And the truth of the matter is that work can never set you free – whether you are in a Nazi concentration camp, a CEO of a billion-dollar company, a dedicated farmer, an Oxbridge or Ivy-league student, or in ministry. If you are looking to your work for freedom, even good or sacrificial works, you too are tormenting yourself. *The only work that can set us free is the work of Jesus Christ at Calvary and his life of perfect obedience to his heavenly Father.*

In justification is a freedom that we don't realise we have. The Christians in Galatia were the same, Paul wrote to them, 'For freedom Christ has set us free; stand firm therefore, and do not submit again to a yoke of slavery' (Gal. 5:1). Like Gemma, many of us still sit in our broken fetters, shackled to our desire to be acceptable and loved. Perhaps we beat ourselves up to be accepted by God, ourselves, or others? Do you work slavishly in church, at your career, on your appearance for acceptance when we already have it through Christ? This doctrine silences our critics, whether trolls online or in our head. Whether Satan or self. There is no guilt. Justification is the awesome gospel truth that we are totally forgiven and accepted in Christ.[11] There is no need for our legalism or any works-based spirituality.

One might ask why it is necessary for God to declare us righteous? Could we not believe like the Catholic church, that righteousness is infused as God makes us holy? Here, justification is given only in and through the perfecting work of sanctification. Sanctification is then mixed with justification, and grace is given on account of good works (a misinterpretation of James 2:14-26).[12] This opposes the biblical view of the reformers completely. Luther saw good works as a *fruit* of our righteousness through Christ. Without the declaration of justification we are still distant from God in this life, waiting for sinlessness before full reconciliation and forgiveness is possible. Instead, God justifies His elect *now*, in order to adopt them into His family now, bestowing on them a glorious inheritance.

Conclusion

No matter what comes in this life or the next, we are clothed with our Saviour. 'For the heavens vanish like smoke, the earth will wear out like a garment', but for the believer there is the promise, 'My salvation *will be forever*, and my righteousness *will never be dismayed*' (Isa. 51:6).

Justification brings restoration of relationship like that between God and humanity in the garden of Eden. Now intimate

---

11 Justification is a doctrine that continues to attract much theological debate. One recent position, that has taken ground over the last fifteen years or so, is the idea that justification is not a declaration of righteousness in Christ but Paul is speaking of covenantal, community belonging. This, standing in opposition to the biblical view, is called the New Perspective on Paul.

12 The Canons and Decrees of the Council of Trent, XXIV.

communion can resume. However, this intimacy is even better than that of Eden. No more do we imagine living in our beautiful, perfect garden in daily conversation with a loving God. We are now one with Christ and adopted into the *family* of God, relating to God in a way we have never before.

QUESTIONS

THE MIGHTY EXCHANGE: *JUSTIFICATION*

Therefore, as one trespass led to condemnation for all men, so one act of righteousness leads to justification and life for all men. For as by the one man's disobedience the many were made sinners, *so by the one man's obedience the many will be made righteous* (Rom. 5:18-19).

1. In justification are we 'declared righteous' or 'made righteous'?

2. What role does faith have in our justification?

3. If we belong to Christ, we are innocent and righteous in Him. Why should this give us joy?

4. In what ways are you prone to slip into self-righteousness or self-justification? What truth from this chapter can you wield to fight this?

5. How does justification in Christ set us free?

   Not the labours of my hands
   can fulfil thy law's commands;
   could my zeal no respite know,
   could my tears forever flow,
   all for sin could not atone;
   thou must save, and thou alone.[13]

6. How may the prayer in this hymn change our way of doing ministry?

---

13   Rev. Augustus Toplady, 'Rock of Ages', 1763.

Chapter 10

In My Father's House: Adoption

... in love he predestined us for adoption as sons. (Eph. 1:4-5)

Are you one of those people who dreams of a home that exists only in the deep recesses of your mind? My dream home stands in miles of green countryside not far from the sea. Much time is spent in the colourful nooks of the large garden – with the noisy birds and grasshoppers – as well as indoors. It is not a big house but the windows are tall and wide, flooding every room with airy light in the morning and dancing dappled light as the sun dips behind the trees, in the evening. Only the library is dark and atmospheric, as great old bookcases create a maze of colourful spines in which to hide away with a story. In this house everything is old but beautiful. Every piece of furniture is a dear friend, whispering stories of eras long past. I have been there a long time; I belong there. I know the shape of every crack and flake on the walls, every creak of the stairs. Everything tastes and feels good in this house; the baths, the toast, the tea and the conversation. The beds are fresh and delicious, lingering with the smell of lavender and roses from the garden. The whole place dwells in a realm of peace and rest, where time stands still. This is how I know it doesn't exist on this plane of reality. Each day is a sweet sabbath for mind and soul, and every conversation stirs profound affection and thought. It is more than a forever home: the human yearning for a homeland in which one belongs is met inexpressibly in this place .

I think sometimes there is not even a fine line between homeland fantasies and our yearnings for heaven. Sure, for some the perfect home is only empty materialism and greed. But when people, Christians or non-Christians, speak of a nostalgic pining for a place that they don't even know exists – you wonder whether it is actually a spiritual aching inside. As believers we yearn to be in a home where we belong forever. Looking to the eternal rest of our souls in constant relationship with God, and our siblings in Christ. Contrary to some Christian preachers, heaven is not heaven because its streets are paved with gold and its walls encrusted with jewels (Rev. 21:9-21). Just walk into any jeweller and see whether it fulfils that ache inside your heart. Heaven is heaven because we, God's people, are finally welcomed into a forever family with the Living God. 'And I heard a loud voice from the throne saying, "Behold, the dwelling place of God is with man. He will dwell with them, and they will be his people, and God himself will be with them as their God"' (Rev. 21:3).

The destination of salvation, which we have explored in this book, is full security in our Father's house. This is our inheritance in Christ. Jesus promised this, 'In my Father's house are many rooms. If it were not so, would I have told you that I go to prepare a place for you? And if I go and prepare a place for you, I will come again and will take you to myself, that where I am you may be also' (John 14:2-3). The good news is, however, that this is more than just a promise of heaven. This is our experience *now*. John writes this in his first letter, 'Beloved, we are God's children *now*' (1 John 3:2). Because of our salvation founded upon union with Christ, encompassing all the gospel graces we have outlined; *we are not orphans* (John 14:8). In the doctrine of adoption, we have reached our destination. That is, dwelling with God and – mind-bogglingly – entering into His holy family. Not His organisation ... Not His club or society ... His family! Standing right next to the doctrine of justification is the pronouncement of the Father's adoption of those in Christ to be His children.

WHAT IS ADOPTION?

Adoption is the *instant declaration* of the believer to be a son or daughter of God. Like regeneration and justification, it is not a process but an *immediate act of free grace*. In this declaration a brand-new status is given. Just as the judge's legal pronouncement binds the orphan or unwanted child to a new family; *in divine adoption the justified sinner is graciously welcomed and celebrated into the family of a loving God*.

The relationship between earthly adoption and heavenly adoption is obvious. Just as earthly marriage is a shadow of the heavenly marriage between Christ and the church, the adoption of children into a new family reflects spiritual adoption in Christ. Many Christians who have written on adoption assert that you can't talk about one without the other. Michael A. Milton is one of these. Milton was adopted as a child and has adopted children into His own family. He defines adoption as 'a singular, nonrepeatable, unilateral event based on love, choice, sacrifice, and law, which binds the parties forever by an authoritative decree.'[1] Some call adoption 'the apex of grace and privilege.'[2]

As we draw our exploration into the doctrines of salvation to a close, it makes perfect sense to finish with adoption. This God-truth is Christ rescuing us for a place in His eternal family where we worship God as father. We adore, we worship, and we obey because our God is our loving parent not our judge. We call God father, not simply because it's in the Lord's Prayer. We call Him father because He *is* our Father! This is a crazy, unbelievable truth! What grace! What mercy! When the Lord met Mary Magdalene after His resurrection, He said to her, 'Do not cling to me, for I have not yet ascended to the Father; but go to my brothers and say to them, "*I am ascending to my Father and your Father, to my God and your God*"' (John 20:17). Sure, 'God is not our Father in the same sense as he is the Father of Jesus; we are not God … Jesus is the Son by nature; we are sons by adoption. Jesus is the eternal Son, but God confers sonship upon us in time. But the distinction is not a separation. We are 'fellow heirs with Christ' (Rom. 8:17).'[3]

---

1   Michael A. Milton, *What is the Doctrine of Adoption?* (Phillipsburg, P&R, 2012), 7.

2   Murray, *Redemption*, 134.

3   Frame, *Belief*, 106.

A Beautiful Inheritance

You probably know the story of the skinny, red-haired orphan girl who is adopted by two unmarried siblings. This little girl has only experienced abuse and neglect, but suddenly she receives a new life in a beautiful home called *Green Gables*, amongst the breathless beauty of Prince Edward Island, Canada. Anne Shirley could rightly say, 'The lines have fallen for me in pleasant places; indeed, I have a beautiful inheritance' (Ps. 16:6), as she is welcomed into the home and hearts of Matthew and Marilla Cuthbert.

We are so much like that unwanted orphan! Plain, homely, rebellious and undesirable. And yet because of God's electing love 'the lines have fallen for us in pleasant places', and in adoption we have 'a beautiful inheritance'. When David wrote that Psalm he can't have known the magnitude of what he was saying. He didn't know that he, and every believer, would be given an inheritance of such beauty and magnitude – to be welcomed into God's intimate family! This adoption secures inconceivable privileges in Christ. The Father's 'name put upon' us, we gain access to the 'throne of grace with boldness', to be 'yet never cast off' 'but sealed to the day of redemption', whilst inheriting the promises 'as heirs of everlasting salvation.'[4] This is the inheritance we obtain in Christ (Eph. 1:11). Our union with Him means we are 'admitted to all the liberties and privileges of the sons of God, made heirs of all the promises, and fellow heirs with Christ in glory.'[5]

Adoption and Union

Like all the other subjects of our chapters, we should not think of adoption apart from union with Christ. Murray says that

---

4   Westminster Confession of Faith 12.

5   Westminster Larger Catechism 74.

'union with Christ reaches its zenith in adoption.'[6] You see, without union with Christ we have no business coming into the family of God. Without union with Christ salvation cannot be applied. Adoption can only occur if it follows the transforming experience of new birth or regeneration. 'The sinner is given a new heart and a new spirit and there begins a great process of renewal which will ensure that one day we come to share fully in the nature of our adoptive Father.'[7] Without regeneration it would be unsuitable for us to be children of God since we would still be dead in our sin. Without justification and faith, we stand in front of God as His enemy – guilty and condemned. And without the Spirit's continuing work of sanctification we would be unfit for God's family.

All these gospel graces which are applied by the Spirit, are essential for us to arrive at our Father's house safe and secure. In the covenant of salvation ordained by the Trinity, it was given to the Holy Spirit to seal this adoption (Eph. 1:13-15). It is the Holy Spirit who binds Christ to the believer and the believer to Christ. He is the one who applies Christ's atoning death and the victory of His resurrection to the one with faith (Gal. 3:2-6). And indwelling inside of the believing woman, the Holy Spirit powerfully declares the Father's adoption. For we are 'in the Spirit' and 'all who are led by the Spirit of God are sons [and daughters] of God' (Rom. 8:9, 14).

Chosen sons and daughters

We saw them, we chose them, we took them in and we waited ... And then the phone call came. It finally happened. All the moments since

---

6   Murray, *Redemption*, 170.

7   Macleod, *Faith*, 153.

> *this precious child had been placed in our home culminated in one final moment, the judge has declared, 'Adopted!' Now they are ours!*

Beth, who wrote these words, and her husband Jon have adopted three children and their hearts wait to hear that declaration for another two whom they love dearly. Beth has five children in her home, *all chosen*. Adoption is the destination of election (not the final destination – that would be glorification). As we think back to our first chapter, we can see that election and the Godhead's plan of salvation all took place for the end result of adoption. We know this from Ephesians, 'As he chose us in him before the foundation of the world, that we should be holy and blameless before him. *In love he predestined us for adoption as sons through Jesus Christ*' (Eph. 1:4-5). Beth knows the correlation between election and adoption, she and Jon chose their children and then persevered through interviews, processes and forms, and then finally, the initial election brings forth fruit. The declaration of adoption is given: the child is theirs!

Iain and Rachel experienced something similar:

> A phone call we received in June was the culmination of at least 18 months of hopes and prayers … the judge had declared that our son was legally part of our family. He had been in our care almost from the moment he was born. We had picked him up from the hospital eight months before this as his foster carers. Then two months later our status changed to 'adoptive parents'. Yet the fact we had regular contact with the social workers was a reminder to us that legally he was still cared for by the state. Every time we filled out a form, and had to write a surname that wasn't ours next to his first name, made us long for the day when things would change. When the phone call came, we were overjoyed! We were full of thanks, relief, and excitement. We were truly, officially one family! We took great pride in contacting places like the doctor's surgery to have his

name changed – we wanted the world to know he was legally ours!

WHAT IS ADOPTION?

Our spiritual adoption is also a legal declaration where our name changes and we become members of God's family. The Westminster Larger Catechism defines it as 'an act of the free grace of God, in and for his only Son Jesus Christ, whereby all those that are justified are received into the number of his children, *have his name put upon them*.'[8] Adoption is much like justification, it is a change of legal state not of character. Adoption depends upon the event of justification. Our adoption is given directly because of Christ's justifying work, and just as with justification, Scripture speaks of adoption in a legal sense. 'But when the fullness of time had come, God sent forth his Son, born of woman, born under the law, to redeem those who were under the law, so that we might receive adoption as sons' (Gal. 4:4-5).

To receive adoption means a change in relation to our standing with God. Adoption is 'bringing sinners into an inheritance instead of the punishment due to them.'[9] We are removed from Adam's belt, hanging there as children or sons of disobedience and of wrath, but are then transferred onto the belt of Christ, because of His righteousness, and admitted into His family. Instead we are accepted in Christ, or the New King James Version says God 'made us accepted in the Beloved' (Eph. 1:6). Our justification brings such acceptance that we are added to God's family, testifying to the power and significance of the justification that Christ gives us.

---

8   Westminster Larger Catechism 74 [emphasis mine].

9   Frame, *Belief*, 965.

Already children?

In one sense we are already God's children. Humankind are the sons and daughters of God because God made them. As the prophet Malachi said, 'Have we not all one Father? Has not one God created us' (Mal. 2:10)? Paul makes this point to the people of Athens in Acts, 'In him we live and move and have our being ... For we are indeed his offspring' (Acts 17:24, 28). We are daughters of God not only through creation but beyond this – because we have been spiritually adopted in Christ.

Even being a Jew – the Lord called Israel His Son (Ex. 4:22) – doesn't secure salvation. Paul says you must belong to Christ *first* to be a child of Abraham, 'If you are Christ's, then you are Abraham's offspring, heirs according to promise' (Gal. 3:29). In Christ we find the *ultimate adoption*; an eternal adoption of grace. Knowing God as our Creator or as a Father of our Jewish nation is not enough.

Love we don't believe

God is so generous in His covenant love for us. In the Old Testament we see God adopt two alien or Gentile women. The first is a sex worker and her name is Rahab (Josh. 6:25), and another is a widow, Ruth (Ruth 1-4). Rahab is adopted into the family of Israel. Ruth is adopted into the covenant royal family from which Jesus Christ came.[10] The Lord continues His fatherly love by adopting a whole people in His Son. 'See what kind of love the Father has given to us, that we should be called children of God; and so we are' (1 John 3:1).

Most of us are Gentiles. We might be past sex workers, we might be widows, we might be any and all types of women but because of God's great love He has brought us into His family.

---

10   Milton, *Adoption*, 15-16.

He is now truly our Father. John writes, 'Beloved, we are God's children now' (1 John 3:2).

God's fatherly love is too good to believe and I think actually many of us don't believe it. Do you have a warped view of the fatherhood of God? Do you unconsciously confuse our Heavenly Father to mean He is actually 'heavenly', 'other' or 'aloof'? This adoption is spiritual but it is real. It was the sovereign God's intention in ancient days, that 'to all who did receive him, who believed in his name, he gave the right to become children of God, who were born, not of blood nor of the will of the flesh nor of the will of man, but of God' (John 1:12-13). We don't need to have experienced a problematic father-daughter relationship in our childhood to disbelieve the fatherhood of God – most of us are there already. Perhaps because we instinctively know we're not worthy. We need to preach adoption in Christ to ourselves and live as heirs not slaves. Milton helpfully corrects our thinking, adoption is not an identity, 'I am not an "adopted person." Rather, I *was* adopted.'[11] We must not 'elevate bloodline over covenant.'[12] We are sons and daughters of God not 'adopted of God'. The adoption is final. We must claim our identity as daughters of a living and loving God. Did not the God of the Ages hunt you out in election, sending His Son to ransom you, in order to make you His own?

Not Slaves

Adoption is a truth we have neglected. Contemporary Christians struggle with backsliding, apathy, spiritual depression and lack of assurance. Many of these problems relate to us living as orphans, or worse still, slaves. We are spiritually malnourished. The Apostle Paul had to deal with this spiritual malnutrition too. He

---

11   *Ibid*, 7.

12   *Ibid*, 8.

encourages the New Testament churches with the objective truth of their adoption, 'For you did not receive the spirit of slavery to fall back into fear, but you have received the Spirit of adoption as sons, by whom we cry, "Abba! Father!"' (Rom. 8:15). 'And because you are sons, God has sent the Spirit of his Son into our hearts, crying, "Abba! Father!" So you are no longer a slave, but a son, and if a son, then an heir through God' (Gal. 4:6-7).

John Piper picks up on this teaching encouraging believers that they must not live as slaves but as sons. He says, 'You are no longer slaves who do not know what the Father is up to. You are in the big house. Your slavery is over. You may walk into the Father's study at any time and interrupt him.'[13] This reminds me of when my girls were all very young and not yet at school. Now and then they would take turns to sneak up stairs to see daddy in his study. Tom had a policy of welcoming them and putting them on his knee. He always wanted to be available to his children.

We too enjoy this welcoming availability with our Father in heaven. We are not penniless orphans. We are not slaves. We are not isolated, alone, and oppressed. We are free, justified, daughters of God and heirs of an awesome inheritance that can neither spoil or fade (Gal. 4:7, 1 Pet. 1:4). This inheritance is full communion with our glorious Triune God in a heavenly home, where the architect is God (Heb. 11:10). But it is also rule over the whole of renewed creation (Matt. 5:5, Rev. 3:21). We should give thanks that we have been qualified in Christ to share in this inheritance (Col. 1:12). We are no longer timid slaves. We have been given the Spirit of adoption and so can live with spiritual brawn and confidence (2 Tim. 1:7, NASB).

---

13   Ask Pastor John [July 17, 2019] *How do I live like a Son Rather than a Slave?*

Hope for today

When we feel hurt, betrayed or disappointed by our earthly parents, perhaps in their lack of love towards us, we can cling to our heavenly Father who will hold and sweetly comfort us with His everlasting covenantal love. Recently British musician Elton John expressed that in all his fame and success he still seeks his father's approval, though his father has been dead for thirty years.[14] We have no need for any performance-earned acceptance from our heavenly Father. Christ has secured full approval on our behalf. Instead we can, in all vulnerability and helplessness, depend and rest *fully* on our heavenly Father.

In this doctrine we also find hope in the pain of discipline from the Lord. He disciplines us in love *because* we are His children. 'Have you forgotten the exhortation that addresses you as sons? "My son, do not regard lightly the discipline of the Lord, nor be weary when reproved by him. For the Lord disciplines the one he loves, and chastises every son whom he receives"' (Heb. 12:5-6). Do you know a strained relationship with your heavenly Father because of sin? Although there is distance there is still filial relationship. We can never be disowned! This gives us comfort and confidence to return to Him in repentance and humility. Even in times of sore discipline we can say with Gregory Nazianzen, the early church father, 'My Trinity!' because of our security in Christ.[15]

One day we will be home for good. But our status as children of God gives us hope now. 'For we know that the whole creation has been groaning together in the pains of childbirth until now. And not only the creation, but we ourselves, who have the firstfruits of the Spirit, groan inwardly as we wait eagerly for

---

14   https://www.bbc.co.uk/news/entertainment-arts-50003238

15   Gregory Nazianzen. *Oratio* 38, 8.

adoption as sons, the redemption of our bodies' (Rom. 8:22-23). We wait eagerly for this adoption because 'He will wipe away every tear from their eyes, and death shall be no more, neither shall there be mourning, nor crying, nor pain anymore, for the former things have passed away' (Rev. 21:4). We have hope because, in all the groanings of suffering and sin in this life, we will one day be brought to the family homeland. This is the inheritance we wait for! 'The one who conquers will have this heritage, and I will be his God and he will be my son' (Rev. 21:7).

Conclusion

Beth told me of that moment she was told adoption had been declared: 'I could sing. I could weep. I sink to my knees and cry out to God as my heart explodes with gratitude and praise.' We too should be levelled with thankfulness and praise at this endless grace. We will never be disowned by our Heavenly Father. We are co-heirs with Christ and the Father looks upon us with the same tenderness as He sees His beloved Son. We are daughters accepted in the Beloved.

And yet Beth's words of joy are those of the parent, not the adopted child. Sister-in-Christ, remember that the Lord rejoices over you His daughter! Believe what you read in Scripture. Know the Father's love for you. In trial and fatigue enjoy the truth and majesty of the mighty mountain of adoption by resting in His covenantal embrace. Through our Redeemer Jesus Christ, 'justified by His unalterable decree', you are a daughter, forever![16]

---

16   Milton, *Adoption*, 20.

Questions

In My Father's House: *Adoption*

'The believer's adoption exists from the beginning of his [or her] regenerate life. But as with many of God's other blessings, there is in adoption an *already* and a *not yet*. Although we are already sons and daughters of God, we await a higher fulfilment of our adoption.'[17]

1. Why is the doctrine of adoption not just for heaven?

2. On what ground are believers 'co-heirs' with Christ (Rom. 8:17)?

3. What does the doctrine of adoption tell us about the character or attributes of God?

4. Look at the chapter again. In what ways are justification and adoption similar?

5. How does our spiritual adoption change our prospect of death?

6. How can we as Christian women look forward to going home to our Father's house?

7. Share one truth that you have learnt from reading this book. How can it shape your life?

---

17   Frame, *Belief*, 976.

Conclusion

But far be it from me to boast except in the cross
of our Lord Jesus Christ. (Gal. 6:14)

This is just the beginning! We leave the believer safe and secure in
the arms of a heavenly Father, but what about being made holy
and pure by the Spirit; or the power to persevere in trial; or
the part of the Church, the Bride of Christ or our future glory?
Other books in *The Good Portion* series continue with these great
truths.

This exploration has only been an introduction. We have only touched the surface, like a stone skimming across the water. Like that stone, we have bounded from one mighty doctrine to another, aware of great depths below. I hope you will dive deeper and that this introduction has whetted your appetite. Do check out the bibliography for recommended dive spots. When Paul wrote his golden chain of salvation in Romans chapter 8, he understood as we have seen, the perfect blending and connecting gospel graces of the Holy Trinity worked out in the life of the believer (Rom. 8:30). We have seen how one grace flows from another. Each distinct yet inseparable from the others in the chain. All are spokes of a wheel meeting in the hub of our union with the crucified and risen Christ.

We have said many times that our salvation is a person – King Jesus! All of our redemption is wrapped up in Him, His beauty and His sufficiency. Jesus Christ is the only one who can rescue us. He alone is 'the Way, and the Truth, and the Life' (John 14:6). Let us boast in no other but Him.

Acknowledgments

Thanks goes to Angela Brand, Lucy Beale, Rhona Black, Alison Pomeroy and Fiona Steward – sisters in Christ who gave their time to read parts of the manuscript. Great thanks to Kate MacKenzie and Rosanna Burton of Christian Focus for inviting me to be a part of *The Good Portion* project. Thanks to my in-house editor Anne Norrie and to series editor Keri Folmar in her constant encouragement – in you I find a kindred spirit.

I am grateful to the Rev. Matthew Rees for unwittingly providing a powerful introduction, and Iain and Rachel, Beth and Jon for sharing something of their adoption journeys.

Above all, as always, my gratitude to my resident theologian, editor, champion and barista, Thomas Brand. Words cannot express my thanks to God for you.

> Not to us, O LORD, not to us, but to your name give glory. For the sake of your steadfast love and your faithfulness (Ps. 115:1).

Selected Bibliography

Augustine of Hippo. *De Trinitate.*

Aquinas, Thomas. *Summa Theologica.*

Calvin, John. *Institutes of the Christian Religion: Calvin's Own 'Essentials' Edition* (Edinburgh: Banner of Truth, 2014).

Calvin, John. *Institutes of the Christian Religion.* Trans. Ford Lewis Battles; ed. John T. McNeill (Philadelphia: Westminster Press, 1960).

Bavinck, Herman. *Reformed Dogmatics* (Grand Rapids, MI: 2006).

Berkhof, L. *Systematic Theology* (London: Banner of Truth, 1969).

Brand, Natalie. *Complementarian Spirituality: Reformed Women and Union with Christ* (Eugene: Wipf & Stock, 2013).

Demarest, Bruce. *The Cross and Salvation: The Doctrine of Salvation* [Foundations of Evangelical Theology] (Wheaton, IL: Crossway, 2006).

Donnelly, Edward. *Heaven and Hell* (Edinburgh: Banner of Truth, 2001).

Frame, John. *Systematic Theology: An Introduction to Christian Doctrine* (Phillipsburg, NJ: P&R, 2013).

Gaffin, Richard B. *The Centrality of the Resurrection: A Study in Paul's Soteriology* (Grand Rapids, MI: Baker, 1993).

Jeffery, Steve. Mike Ovey, and Andrew Sach. *Pierced for our Transgressions: Rediscovering the Glory of Penal Substitution* (Leicester: Inter-Varsity Press, 2007).

Kelly, Douglas F. *Systematic Theology* [Vol. 2]: *The Beauty of Christ: A Trinitarian Vision* (Fearn, Ross-shire: Mentor, 2014).

Letham, Robert. *The Lord's Supper: Eternal Word in Broken Bread* (Phillipsburg, NJ: P&R Publishing, 2001).

Letham, Robert. *The Westminster Assembly: Reading its Theology in Historical Context* (Phillipsburg, NJ: P&R Publishing, 2009).

Letham, Robert. *The Work of Christ* (Nottingham: Inter-Varsity Press, 1993).

Luther, Martin. *Works* (Saint Louis: Concordia Publishing, 1963).

Macleod, Donald. *A Faith to Live By: Understanding Christian Doctrine* (Fearn, Ross-shire: Christian Focus, 2010).

MacLeod, Donald. *Christ Crucified: Understanding the Atonement* (Nottingham: Inter-Varsity Press, 2014).

Milton, Michael A. *What is the Doctrine of Adoption?* (Phillipsburg, NJ: P&R, 2012).

Murray, John. *Redemption: Accomplished and Applied* (London: Banner of Truth, 1961).

Pink, Arthur W. *The Holy Spirit* (Grand Rapids, MI: Baker, 1978).

Rutherford, Samuel. *The Loveliness of Christ* (Edinburgh: The Banner of Truth, 2007).

Spurgeon, C. H. *Faith* (New Kensington, PA: Whitaker House, 1995).

Warfield, B. B. *Biblical Doctrines* (Edinburgh: Banner of Truth, 1988).

Scripture Index